100

THINGS TO DO IN
RHODE
ISLAND
BEFORE YOU
DIE

Photo credit: Bob Curley

100

THINGS TO DO IN
RHODE
ISLAND
BEFORE YOU
DIE

BOB CURLEY

REEDY PRESS

Copyright © 2019 by Reedy Press, LLC
Reedy Press
PO Box 5131
St. Louis, MO 63139, USA
www.reedypress.com

No part of this publication may be reproduced or transmitted in any form or by any means, electronic or mechanical, including photocopy, recording, or any information storage and retrieval system, without permission in writing from the publisher.

Permissions may be sought directly from Reedy Press at the above mailing address or via our website at www.reedypress.com.

Library of Congress Control Number: 2019936699

ISBN: 9781681062112

Design by Jill Halpin

Printed in the United States of America
19 20 21 22 23   5 4 3 2 1

Please note that websites, phone numbers, addresses, and company names are subject to change or cancellation. We did our best to relay the most accurate information available, but due to circumstances beyond our control, please do not hold us liable for misinformation. When exploring new destinations, please do your homework before you go.

DEDICATION

To Christine, who is always willing to go (and usually, walk) the extra mile in pursuit of my crazy story ideas; and to Christopher and Shannon for fueling my childlike sense of adventure, even if they're not kids themselves anymore!

Standup paddleboarding on the Narrow River
(Photo credit: Katherine Gendreau)

CONTENTS

● ●

• •

• •

Culture and History

• •

• •

PREFACE

Rhode Island is a little place, so you might think it would be a challenge to come up with 100 experiences you absolutely, positively must have before shuffling off your mortal coil. On the contrary: the 50th-largest state is so rich in the unique, the extraordinary, and the delicious that—were there time, and perhaps another title to the series—I could have easily added 100 more attractions, events, and culinary and cultural delights. Nonetheless, I've tried to curate a collection of experiences that not only capture the essence of the Ocean State, but will also truly make your life richer for having enjoyed them. I hope you get as much pleasure reading this book—and, more important, getting out and making your own memories—as I had writing it. Thanks, and see you on the Rhode!

ACKNOWLEDGMENTS

Special thanks to the Providence Warwick Convention and Visitors Bureau, especially Kristen Adamo and Christina Robbio, Andrea McHugh and Evan Smith at Discover Newport, Louise Bishop and Faye Pantazopoulos of the South County Tourism Council, Jessica Willi at Block Island Tourism, Annie Sherman Luke of Newport Life, Grace Lentini, Kim Knox Beckius, the Blackstone Valley Tourism Council, the Rhode Island Commerce Corp., and all of the other travel writers and local experts who contributed their bucket-list ideas to this book. You're all to die for!

• •

Photo credit: Grace Lentini

FOOD AND DRINK

STUFF YOURSELF SILLY
AT THE NORDIC

How much do you think you can eat at once? Are you someone who can hold out all day in anticipation of a big meal, or do you just want an opportunity to sidle up to a table overflowing with the best of everything? If either is true, splurge for a dinner at the Nordic, a lakeside buffet restaurant in rural Charlestown that serves unlimited lobster, filet mignon, prime rib, spare ribs, and a cornucopia of other entrées, sides, and desserts. It's not cheap—dinner (served Friday, Saturday, and Sunday from the end of April until mid December) costs more than one hundred dollars per adult—but you can eat as much as you want of anything you want for two hours. It's not something your waistline will thank you for doing on a regular basis, but it's definitely a meal you should experience at least once.

The Nordic
178 East Pasquiset Trl., Charlestown, RI 02813
(401) 783-4515
thenordic.com

TIP
Use the beach volleyball court on the property to burn off some calories before you get seated, and stick around after your meal for live music lakeside during the summer.

DELIGHT IN GREASY GOODNESS
AT YE OLDE ENGLISH FISH & CHIPS

Woonsocket is about as far from the ocean as you can get in Rhode Island, yet strangely it's the best place to get fish and chips, the quintessential New England seaside meal. A restaurant that has seemingly been around forever (almost a century, in this case), Ye Olde English Fish & Chips still uses the original batter recipe from 1922, and, although lard has been replaced by vegetable oil for frying, the Market Square landmark stays true to its simple promise of serving the most authentic English-style fish and chips this side of the Atlantic. The fries are still hand peeled and cut, the fish is fresh, and the no-nonsense atmosphere signals that it's all about the food at this northern Rhode Island institution.

Ye Olde English Fish & Chips
25 South Main St., Woonsocket, RI 02895
(401) 762-3637
yeoldeenglishfishandchips.com

TIP
For a change of pace, try the fish cakes—deep-fried fish between two slices of potato—another authentic English recipe.

ATTEND
A MAY BREAKFAST

For more than 150 years, churches and community groups in Rhode Island have opened their doors to friends and strangers for social foodie fundraisers called May breakfasts. The Oak Lawn Community Baptist Church in Cranston is credited with hosting the first May breakfast back in 1867 and continues the tradition to this day, laying out a family-style spread that includes Rhode Island standards like johnnycakes and clam cakes alongside more common breakfast items like ham and eggs and brunch-y food like apple pie and cornbread. Proceeds from the first May breakfast went to build a new church, and the dozens of other groups that now host these traditional spring gatherings also use them to raise money, so you can do some good while filling your tummy with homemade treats.

Oak Lawn Community Baptist Church
229 Wilbur Ave., Cranston, RI 02921
(401) 944-0864
olcbaptistchurch.com

TIP
Check local newspapers, magazines, websites, and Facebook for information on May breakfasts, some of which actually take place in April as well.

EAT A HOT LOBSTER ROLL [OR TWO]
AT THE EASTON'S BEACH SNACK BAR

The traditional New England lobster roll is lobster meat tossed in mayo and some diced celery and served chilled on a warm roll. It's delicious, but for sheer indulgence it can't hold a claw to the hot lobster roll. You'll find the latter in fewer places, but if you only get to have one, then have the hot lobster roll served at the Easton's Beach Snack Bar. Located on Newport's "First Beach," the snack bar is actually best known for its twin lobster rolls—that's right, two toasted hot dog rolls filled with lobster meat and drizzled with melted butter. Even with a side of fries it's less than twenty dollars—unquestionably the greatest, most succulently indulgent crustacean deal you'll find in Rhode Island.

Easton's Beach Snack Bar
175 Memorial Blvd., Newport, RI 02840
(401) 855-1910
eastonsbeach.com

TIP

Take a spin on the Easton's Beach carousel—located in the same building as the snack bar—before or after your lobster feast. At three dollars a ride it's another one of Newport's best bargains!

FEAST ON ITALIAN FOOD
ON FEDERAL HILL

Federal Hill is Providence's Little Italy, and while some non-Italian restaurants have filtered in over the years, it's still the go-to location for great pizza, pasta, and meeting the local paisanos. Beloved by generations of Rhode Islanders, the restaurants on the Hill include the white-tablecloth Joe Marzilli's Old Canteen and the no-frills Angelo's Civita Farnese, known for its big portions and low prices. Others—such as Siena, Zooma, and Cassarino's—put a more contemporary spin on the classics. In warm weather, the place to be is DePasquale Square, where cafés surround a fountain topped with a stylized pinecone (a symbol of welcome) and you can browse through old-school Italian delis and butcher shops or nibble on a pastry from the nearby Scialo Bros. Bakery, in business since 1916.

federalhillprov.com

TIP
Federal Hill is at its most ethnic during the annual Feast of St. Joseph, which includes a celebratory procession and snacking on traditional zeppoles.

TAP INTO YOUR SWEET SIDE
AT THE SPRING HILL SUGAR HOUSE

Like the rest of New England, Rhode Island has cold weather and lots of maple trees—the perfect recipe for making maple syrup. At Exeter's Spring Hill Sugar House, you can see how the sweet delicious syrup gets from tree to bottle—a labor-intensive process that includes tapping countless trees, collecting the sap in buckets, and boiling off the water content until the sap becomes syrup. Liquid maple syrup is worth far more than crude oil, and you'll understand why when you learn that it takes forty gallons of sap to make one gallon of maple syrup. Spring Hill Sugar House owner Gibby Fountain will demonstrate how it's done and happily sell you the finished product for your morning pancakes and waffles.

Spring Hill Sugar House
522 Gardner Rd., Exeter, RI 02822
(401) 788-7431
facebook.com/spring-hill-sugar-house-130250857046253

TIP
Bring cash if you want to buy some maple syrup or honey from the farm—Spring Hill Sugar House doesn't accept credit cards.

TAKE A COUNTRY DRIVE FOR ICE CREAM
AT GRAY'S

Tiverton Four Corners is a charming coastal New England crossroads dotted with eighteenth- and nineteenth-century homes now converted to shops, restaurants, art galleries, and—most important—Gray's Ice Cream. A local landmark, Gray's has been scooping out dozens of homemade flavors since 1923, including its famous coffee ice cream and seasonal treats like Indian pudding, a traditional New England dessert in frozen form. The creamery started as a casual affair, with founder Annie Gray selling ice cream from the back window of her house, but while the business and the building have expanded in the near century since, you'll still find big crowds of people waiting to choose their favorites among the forty flavors on almost any day the sun is shining—a sure sign of quality at a place that's not particularly close to anything.

Gray's Ice Cream
16 East Rd., Tiverton, RI 02878
(401) 624-4500
graysicecream.com

TIP

Slake your craving and beat the crowds by visiting Gray's in the off-season: unlike most other ice cream stands in Rhode Island, it's open 365 days a year.

GET SPIRITED
AT SONS OF LIBERTY

Sons of Liberty hit the spirits scene with a splash half a decade ago by winning national honors for its pumpkin-flavored whiskey, and the Peace Dale distillery has only gotten better in the years since. You may know that all whiskey starts from beer, but usually it's a low-quality brew useful only for a quick move to the distilling stage. Sons of Liberty departed from this model by brewing diverse and high-quality beer as the base of its signature single malt whiskies such as Uprising and Battle Cry, and the accolades have continued to flow in. Located in a former mill building, the distillery features tastings, games, live music, and visiting food trucks, and since Sons of Liberty finally circled back to brewing beer for public consumption, you can sample that when you visit too.

Sons of Liberty Spirits Company
1425 Kingstown Rd., South Kingstown, RI 02879
(401) 284-4006
solspirits.com

TIP
Sons of Liberty also makes a line of canned cocktails called Loyal 9 that you can find in local stores. They come in three flavors: lemonade, half & half (an Arnold Palmer, basically), and mixed berry lemonade.

DRINK A CABINET
AT DELEKTA PHARMACY

Drink a cabinet, you say? Sounds weird, but in Rhode Island "cabinet" is an old-fashioned term for a milkshake, and the smooth ice cream drinks whipped up at Delekta Pharmacy in Warren are among the best. The coffee cabinet—made with homemade coffee syrup (a Rhode Island specialty), ice cream, and milk—is the traditional favorite, but you can also get one in vanilla, chocolate, or other tempting flavors, like pumpkin, available in the fall. Ice cream and root beer floats are other options. The Delekta family ended the pharmacy side of their business a few years ago, but visitors can still see the vintage drug bottles on the wood-paneled walls and admire the culinary accoutrements of one of the oldest soda fountains in the state.

Delekta Pharmacy
496 Main St., Warren, RI 02885
(401) 245-6767
facebook.com/pages/category/ice-cream-shop/delekta-pharmacy-30251397602

TIP
If you're not an "eat dessert first" type, start with lunch at nearby Eli's Kitchen, which has great po'boys and Cubano sandwiches.

PUNCH YOUR PASSPORT
ON THE RHODE ISLAND
BREWERY TRAIL

There's not a pot of gold at the end of the Rhode Island brewery trail—but there is a free glass of beer. The Rhode Island Brewers Guild sponsors the Rhode Island Brewery Passport, which beer lovers can use as a guide to the state's twenty-plus independent breweries and get a stamp from each one they visit. Visit seven breweries and you'll get a Brewer's Guild pint glass; check out fourteen, and you'll quaff your way to a cool hat. The most coveted award of all awaits those who visit twenty-two breweries: you'll get a special bottle of beer brewed exclusively each year for Passport holders. I can't think of a better reason to make the rounds of Rhode Island's diverse and exceptional breweries, from the award-winning Whalers in Peace Dale (try their flagship Rise, an American pale ale) to the farm-to-glass IPAs at Tilted Barn in North Kingstown and the Rhode Island-themed lineup from Revival Brewing Company's acclaimed brewmaster, Sean Larkin.

Rhode Island Brewers Guild
293 JT Connell Hwy., Newport, RI 02840
ribrewersguild.org

TIP

Looking to sample a wide range of local beers in one sitting? Pay a visit to The Guild in Pawtucket, a brewery, taphouse, and performance space where eight regional breweries produce their draughts.

SAVOR THE FLAVOR
OF HARTLEY'S ORIGINAL PORK PIES

French meat pies are a tradition in northern Rhode Island thanks to the area's large population of French Canadian families who migrated south to work in the mills along the Blackstone River during the Industrial Revolution. Hartley's pork pies are in the same culinary tradition but with different roots: this tiny shop in Lincoln serves up English-style pies—not just pork but also chicken, beef, and salmon varieties. Each pie costs under three dollars and can be finished in under five bites but is so dense that a serving of two is more than enough for lunch. Generous portions of meat swimming in thick gravy reside in flaky crusts made from lard: it's not health food, but it's still made in-house from scratch using a century-old recipe, and I dare you not to eat every last savory crumb and lick your fingers afterward.

Hartley's Original Pork Pies
871 Smithfield Ave., Lincoln, RI 02865
(401) 726-1295
facebook.com/hartleysoriginalporkpiesfallriver

TIP
Arrive early: Hartley's is open Wednesday to Friday at 7 a.m. and closes by 2 p.m. or whenever they run out of pies.

TRY SOME
STRIPPED-DOWN BAKERY PIZZA

You know how you can tell that a pizza sauce and crust are good? When they taste great even without a coating of cheese. It may sound like sacrilege, but cheese-less pizza is a Rhode Island tradition that is a staple at backyard picnics and kids' birthday parties. The treat—alternatively known as "pizza strips" and "bakery pizza"—comes in broad sheets cut into rectangles; it's rarely eaten as a meal, but rather as a savory snack food served unheated. The best examples have a crisp bottom crust and a tart and tomatoey sauce generously suffused with olive oil. You can easily find pizza strips at local supermarkets like Dave's Marketplace, but Rhode Islanders also swear by neighborhood Italian bakeries like DePetrillo's in Warwick and D. Palmieri's in Johnston.

TIP

Pizza chips are different than pizza strips—they're round and have cheese—but they're another tasty Rhode Island pizza treat you need to try: get them by the bag at the Original Italian Bakery on Atwood Avenue in Johnston.

INVADE THE HOTEL VIKING ROOFTOP
FOR DRINKS AND DINING

The elegant, brick-faced Hotel Viking has a rich history of hospitality dating back to 1926, and the hotel occupies a lofty spot on Bellevue Avenue in Newport's Historic Hill neighborhood. Take full advantage of the location by heading to the Top of Newport Bar + Kitchen, which hands down has the best views of the city of any public space in town. Order a Dark 'n' Stormy or something bubbly and drink in the views of the historic seaside city and Narragansett Bay, then stick around for a meal or—better yet—book a room. Recurring summer rooftop events include Spirits and Stogies dinners, and the Historic Hotels of America property also makes a great base for exploring Newport.

Hotel Viking
1 Bellevue Ave., Newport, RI 02840
(401) 847-3300
hotelviking.com

TIP

Live music is part of the fun up on the roof, with performers singing and strumming from 6 p.m. to 9 p.m. Wednesday through Saturday.

GET WILD
AT PADDY'S IN WESTERLY

For the few precious months that are summer in New England, Paddy's Beach Club channels a little slice of South Beach, a dash of the Caribbean, and even a taste of Ibiza to create the best beach party in Rhode Island. Bottle service, bikinis, and DJs spinning dance music create the vibe at Tikki Beach, Paddy's private beach club, where you can rent cabanas or day beds and hang out with the young and beautiful. Food and drinks are served day and evening on the outside deck, including a selection of tiki drinks served in themed glasses. Inside, live bands play some nights, while others are reserved for special events that include a popular "foam party," which is just like it sounds: a dance floor that fills with foamy bubbles and progressively wetter and wilder dancers.

Paddy's Beach Club
159 Atlantic Ave., Westerly, RI 02981
(401) 584-0028
paddysbeach.com

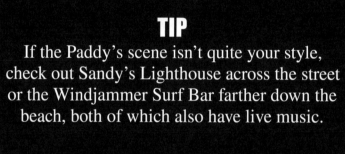

TIP

If the Paddy's scene isn't quite your style, check out Sandy's Lighthouse across the street or the Windjammer Surf Bar farther down the beach, both of which also have live music.

EAT PASTA AND GRAVY
AT MIKE'S KITCHEN

Italian heritage runs deep in Rhode Island, and Federal Hill in Providence is full of fine dining restaurants serving the best cuisine from every region of Italy. Mike's Kitchen in Cranston, by contrast, shares space with a local VFW post. The description may not inspire confidence, and the basic banquet hall decor and wine in fruit glasses doesn't exactly scream "date night." However, the food is both inexpensive and outstanding, and the atmosphere is unvarnished, authentic Rhode Island. House wine is sold by the carafe and comes from the VFW bar (you pay for wine and beer separately from the food). Fuggedabout osso bucco and buffalo ricotta; at Mike's, you want to stick to the classics, like chicken piccata, sole florentine, chicken parmesan, and veal marsala. And the locals say you can't beat the pasta and gravy, either.

Mike's Kitchen
170 Randall St., Cranston, RI 02920
(401) 946-5320
facebook.com/mikeskitchentaborfranchipost

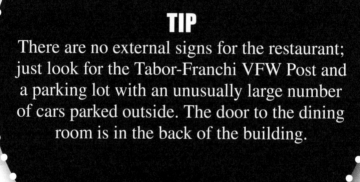

TIP

There are no external signs for the restaurant; just look for the Tabor-Franchi VFW Post and a parking lot with an unusually large number of cars parked outside. The door to the dining room is in the back of the building.

MAKE A
LATE-NIGHT STOP
FOR NEW YORK SYSTEM WIENERS

Every state seems to have a favorite food for filling your belly after a night of revelry—an immediately satisfying infusion of protein that throws concern to the morning after. In Rhode Island, that tasty late-night dish is the hot wiener, a little beef dog that gets expertly lined up on the grill man's arm and topped with mustard, onions, celery salt, and a ground-beef based wiener sauce. If you haven't indulged at Olneyville New York System restaurant at 2:30 a.m., can you even consider yourself a Rhode Islander? Perhaps, but there's no bad time of day to experience this take on the humble hot dog, which has won praise from comfort food guru Guy Fieri and has even snagged a James Beard Award as a classic American food.

Olneyville New York System
18 Plainfield St., Providence, RI 02909
(401) 621-9500
olneyvillenewyorksystem.com

TIP
Olneyville New York System has a second location in Cranston (1012 Reservoir Ave.), and there are also several other restaurants around the state that sell hot wieners.

GO FISH
AT AUNT CARRIE'S

Summer isn't summer in New England without a stop for some fried seafood after a day at the beach, and in Rhode Island Aunt Carrie's has been the place to get your clam cakes and chowdah for generations. The restaurant in Point Judith is a no-frills operation: there's technically a dining room, but in good weather you'll want to snare one of the picnic tables outside. Settle in for a classic New England shore dinner of chowder, clam cakes, steamed clams, fish and chips, or lobster, or opt for comparatively lighter fare like lobster rolls (cold or hot) or the broiled catch of the day. Chase it down with dessert made in-house, like traditional Indian pudding, or save room for ice cream from Aunt Carrie's creamery across the street.

Aunt Carrie's
1240 Ocean Rd., Narragansett, RI 02882
(401) 783-7930
auntcarriesri.com

TIP
For another Rhode Island treat, order some fried doughboys covered in powdered sugar from Iggie's, just down the street.

TOAST THE SUNSET
ON THE COAST GUARD HOUSE DECK

The name Coast Guard House is a bit of a misnomer: the stone building on the edge of Narragansett Bay was built in 1888 by famed architects McKim, Mead & White to house a station of the United States Life-Saving Service, the predecessor of the U.S. Coast Guard. The building in Narragansett Pier has been a restaurant and landmark for decades, but the addition of a roof deck has transformed the Coast Guard House into the best place in the state to sip a summer cocktail as the sun settles over the bay. The bar serves local beer, wine, and cocktails, as well as frozen drinks like a slushy dark 'n' stormy—the ultimate cool-down drink on a warm July evening.

Coast Guard House
40 Ocean Rd., Narragansett, RI 02882
(401) 789-0700
thecoastguardhouse.com

TIP
If the main deck is crowded, there also are bay-facing Adirondack chairs outside on the ground level of the restaurant.

DRINK IN SUMMER
ON THE CASTLE HILL INN'S LAWN

Looking to recapture a little Gilded Age glamor in Newport? Join the well-heeled crowd sipping cocktails on summer afternoons at the Castle Hill Inn, a seaside mansion built in 1875 with unmatched views of Newport Harbor. Rum is the favored spirit to sip in one of the Adirondack chairs scattered around the lawn—try the single-barrel Thomas Tew; it's distilled right here in Newport—but a glass of wine or a gin & tonic goes quite nicely, too. For a more formal experience you can get a table on the outdoor deck, where lunch is served daily and a jazz band livens up Sunday brunch. And of course there's always the option of an overnight stay at the turreted inn, which was once the home of marine biologist Alexander Agassiz.

Castle Hill Inn
590 Ocean Dr., Newport, RI 02840
(401) 849-3800
castlehillinn.com

TIP
Take a short stroll along the cliff in front of the inn to the Castle Hill Lighthouse, a stubby but still-active beacon that has been warning sailors away from the rocks since 1890.

GET INTO A GRILLED PIZZA
AT AL FORNO

How many restaurants can claim to have invented a pizza? If you've ever chomped into a crispy, wood-grilled pizza, you have the founders of Providence's Al Forno, George Germon and Johanne Killeen, to thank. For more than thirty years, Al Forno has been serving its original Grilled Pizza Margarita, with a San Marzano-based tomato sauce and a three-cheese blend (fontina, Parmesan Reggiano, and Romano), basil, parsley, and fresh scallions spread over homemade pizza dough and grilled at high heat over a charcoal brazier. For a little more than twenty dollars, you're biting into a slice of culinary history that has stood the test of time and inspired imitators all over the world, and you can only get the original at Al Forno's restaurant in downtown Providence.

Al Forno
577 South Water St., Providence, RI 02903
(401) 273-9760
alforno.com

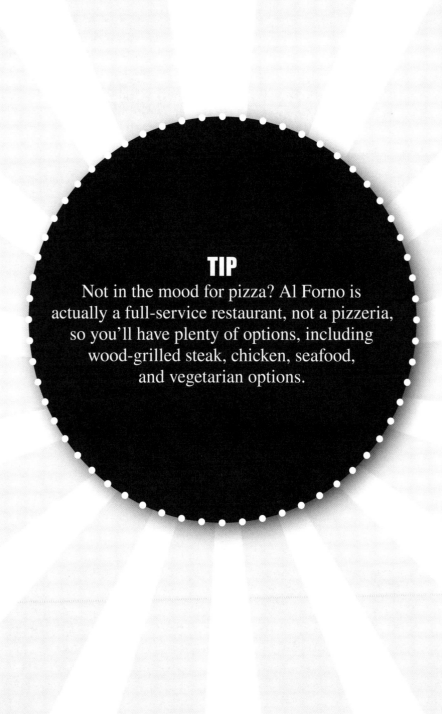

TIP
Not in the mood for pizza? Al Forno is
actually a full-service restaurant, not a pizzeria,
so you'll have plenty of options, including
wood-grilled steak, chicken, seafood,
and vegetarian options.

TAKE YOUR FLOCK
TO WRIGHT'S FARM

Family-style chicken dinners are a northern Rhode Island tradition, and for half a century the place to go for all-you-can-eat roasted chicken, iceberg salad, pasta and tomato "gravy," french fries, and rolls is Wright's Farm in Harrisville. It's not fancy, but the roasted chicken comes out hot and juicy and nobody ever leaves the table hungry. Not feeling chicken? The restaurant also offers the option of ordering a fourteen-ounce sirloin steak— it's just a single portion, though. By the way, "family style" doesn't mean only "your family"—guests are seated at long communal tables, and heaping plates are passed along from diner to diner. Taken in the right spirit, it's actually a great way to meet people and chat in a relaxed atmosphere where everyone is sharing in a hearty meal.

Wright's Farm
84 Inman Rd., Harrisville, RI 02830
(401) 769-2856
wrightsfarm.com

TIP
If there's a wait for a table, kill some time browsing through the chicken-themed souvenirs, candy, clothing, and jewelry in the restaurant's large gift shop.

DRESS UP FOR BRUNCH
AT THE OCEAN HOUSE

Quite simply the classiest day-starter in the poshest hotel in Rhode Island, brunch at the Ocean House in Watch Hill is the special occasion meal in which to indulge when you'd rather start celebrating in the morning and not at dinner. The fulsome spread includes antipasto, raw bar, omelet, and crepe stations elegantly laid out in the hotel's sunny main dining room, plus soup and salad for starters and a selection of hot breakfast and lunch entrées. Toast the new day with a glass of bubbly and linger over live jazz and a meal that's meant as an event—dress up for the occasion and then enjoy a postprandial stroll on the resort's veranda and down to the beach.

Ocean House
1 Bluff Ave., Watch Hill, RI 02891
(855) 678-0364
oceanhouseri.com

TIP
Feeling romantic? The Ocean House offers a three-course winter fondue dinner for two in a vintage ski gondola on the hotel's North Lawn.

ENJOY BURGERS, BANDS, AND BOCCE
AT THE RATHSKELLER

The Charlestown Rathskeller is a legend that keeps on growing. Founded as a backwoods speakeasy in 1933, the bar retains its original murals of boxing legends like Joe Louis and Max Schmeling and the hand-cut fries that have pleased customers since its earliest days, but the business has expanded beyond its founders' wildest dreams. While still well off the beaten path among the forests and fields of Charlestown, the Rat boasts of having the coldest beer in Rhode Island and definitely has one of the state's best burgers. Outside, the spacious grounds are filled with beach volleyball, horseshoes, and bocce courts, along with a stage and fire pit where live bands perform from spring to fall. If ever there were a bar to find in Rhode Island on a warm summer evening, this is it.

Charlestown Rathskeller
489a Old Coach Rd., Charlestown, RI 02813
(401) 792-1000
thecharlestownrathskeller.com

TIP
Order the fries with the short-rib gravy.
You can thank me when you see me.

EAT THE HOLE THING
AT ALLIE'S DONUTS

There may be no more doughnut-crazy state in the United States than Rhode Island, where you'll find a Dunkin' Donuts on seemingly every street corner and a pair of excellent gourmet doughnut shops (PVDonuts and Knead) in the capital city of Providence. With a tip of the doughnut hole to the newcomers, my favorite remains the old-school Allie's Donuts, which has been boxing up fresh doughnuts and strong coffee in North Kingstown since 1963. Proof that good things come in small packages, Allie's is housed in a dinky building where morning lines frequently snake outside, rain or shine. Dense, warm, and fresh, Allie's doughnuts are worth the wait, and the weight alone demonstrates the difference between these sweet circles of joy and their chain-store counterparts. The Boston cream and chocolate frosted are personal favorites, but you really can't go wrong no matter what your heart's doughnut desire is.

Allie's Donuts
3661 Quaker Ln., North Kingstown, RI 02852
(401) 295-8036
facebook.com/alliesdonuts

TIP

Bring cash along with your patience for waiting in line: Allie's doesn't take credit cards.

GO TO SHELL
AT MATUNUCK OYSTER BAR

To really immerse yourself in a farm-to-table experience, join Matunuck Oyster Bar owner Perry Raso on a free one-hour tour of his oyster farm on nearby Potter's Pond, where you'll learn how the sustainable aquaculture operation keeps the shellfish flowing from their beds to your plate. Then head back to the restaurant to sample some oysters, calamari fresh off the boat from nearby Point Judith, authentic Rhode Island-style quahog chowder, a burger from Sunset Farms, or entrées featuring local seafood accompanied by vegetables from the restaurant's own farm. The raw bar provides the opportunity for grazing (the oyster sampler includes a selection of a dozen local oysters) as well as indulgence (order twelve Matunuck oysters accompanied by a bottle of Veuve Clicquot champagne).

Matunuck Oyster Bar
629 Succotash Rd., South Kingstown, RI 02879
(401) 783-4202
rhodyoysters.com

TIP
Nab a coveted seat on the outdoor deck and you might see a boat sidling up to the dock loaded with just-harvested shellfish destined for the kitchen.

DRINK A DEL'S
ON THE BEACH

Officially, coffee milk is the state drink of Rhode Island. But while we applaud those whose idea of a treat is to pour coffee-flavored syrup in a glass of cow juice, there's no comparison in terms of refreshment on a hot summer day than sipping down a cup of Del's Lemonade. A slushy fruit ice made with real lemon juice and lemon pieces, sugar, and ice, Del's is sold from seasonal roadside stands as well as out of instantly recognizable trucks. Del's also comes in other flavors—watermelon, blueberry, tangerine-orange, grapefruit, pink lemonade, and blueberry— but the lemon is still king. And of course the best place to have a Del's is on the beach—rare is the Rhode Island beach that doesn't have a Del's truck or stand: just "look for the sign of the lemon."

dels.com

TIP
Avoid the dreaded "brain freeze" by squeezing the paper cup and taking the lemon ice in small nibbles, not chunks. It will last longer that way, too.

Steve Earle playing at the Greenwich Odeum
(Photo credit: The Odeum)

MUSIC AND ENTERTAINMENT

SEA A BAND PLAY
AT THE OCEAN MIST

Rhode Island's best beach bar and waterfront live-music venue has stood both the test of time and the ravages of Mother Nature in its thirty-year history. An old-school roadhouse perched on stilts above the pounding waves of the Atlantic Ocean, the Mist offers up a steady stream of music from local and national bands on its indoor stage and serves surprisingly excellent seafood and good old American comfort food on its outdoor deck. Part of the bar's charm is the different ways you can enjoy your time here: start the day with breakfast on the deck, hang out with a beer on the beach, come Monday for taco night (Mexican food is a specialty here), or relax with friends at the bar with no-cover live bands on Sunday Funday. Fridays and Saturdays are when the big names roll in, including reggae legends like Toots and the Maytals and household names like John Popper of Blues Traveler, NRBQ, Deer Tick, and the English Beat.

Ocean Mist
895 Matunuck Beach Rd., Wakefield, RI 02879
(401) 782-3740
oceanmist.net

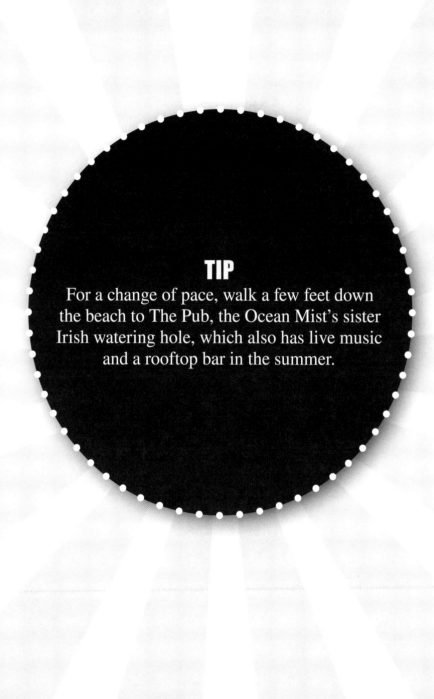

TIP

For a change of pace, walk a few feet down the beach to The Pub, the Ocean Mist's sister Irish watering hole, which also has live music and a rooftop bar in the summer.

ATTEND
THE NEWPORT FOLK AND
JAZZ FESTIVALS

In their sixty-plus years of history, these twin festivals have played host to some of the most memorable musical performances ever, including Bob Dylan's first "electric" show at the Folk Festival in 1965 and landmark shows by Miles Davis and Duke Ellington at the Jazz Festival. The shows are now held a week apart at Fort Adams State Park, drawing tens of thousands of fans on land and a fleet of boats full of people listening for free from Narragansett Bay. There's really no bad time to attend these world-famous festivals, but the kickoff Friday shows are sometimes the best.

newportjazz.org
newportfolk.org

TIP
Keep the beat going between the festivals by attending BridgeFest, which includes a full schedule of shows—including some by performers who also take the Folk or Jazz Fest stage—at local live music venues around Newport.

MAKE A COMEDY CONNECTION
IN EAST PROVIDENCE

You can bank on laughs at East Providence's Comedy Connection (that's a little joke, because the club is located in a former bank building). Other comedy venues have come and gone, but the Comedy Connection has been a funny place to spend a night for decades, hosting nationally famous comedians like Tom Green and D. L. Hughley as well as up-and-coming acts, local comedians, and promising newcomers at the weekly Sunday Showcase. The club has a full bar and serves pizza, appetizers, and quesadillas, and you can get drinks before, during, and after the show. So come make an evening of it—after all, in these trying times, if there's one thing we can all use, it's a good laugh.

Comedy Connection
39 Warren Ave., East Providence, RI 02914
(401) 438-8383
ricomedyconnection.com

TIP
If you go to see a particular local comic, mention it at the door—performers get a few bucks for each person they get to come.

PARTY WITH A YACHTY
IN THE BOOM BOOM ROOM

There's no guarantee that you'll find a mate in the Boom Boom Room, but you'll definitely meet some sailors. Located below the Candy Store at Newport's Clarke Cooke House, the Boom Boom Room has been the place to dance, mix, and mingle with yacht owners (and those who wish they were) since the golden age of disco, and the party still gets plenty hot on summer nights. The ties between the Clarke Cooke House and the boating community run strong: the upstairs restaurant is a hangout for affluent sailors up to and including America's Cup crewmembers, while the Candy Store bar lends its name to an annual superyacht race. Inevitably, however, the action moves down to the basement, where the Boom Boom Room offers pounding dance music and a cramped, dark, yet oddly seductive dive-bar vibe as an antidote to the tonier atmosphere upstairs.

Clarke Cooke House
24 Bannister's Wharf, Newport, RI 02840
(401) 849-2900
clarkecooke.com

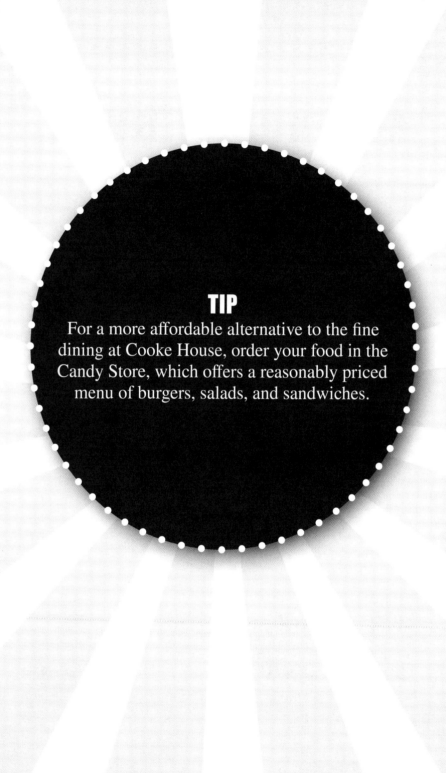

TIP

For a more affordable alternative to the fine dining at Cooke House, order your food in the Candy Store, which offers a reasonably priced menu of burgers, salads, and sandwiches.

MAKE A HAUNTED VISIT
TO THE ZOO

The Roger Williams Park Zoo is worth a visit any time of year to visit the well-cared-for animal residents, take a camel ride, fly over the park on a zipline, feed the giraffes, watch the elephants take a bath, or check out the new Faces of the Rainforest exhibit. But the zoo is at its most memorable around Halloween, when the Wetlands Trail transforms into a spooky spectacle with thousands of carved pumpkins on display. Dedicated crews of volunteers work with knives and scoops to transform pumpkins into sports legends, cartoon characters, movie stars, and superheroes for the annual Jack-O-Lantern Spectacular. As dusk falls each night from early October to early November, the zoo fills with eerie music, flickering lights, and the ghostly outlines of visitors who make the pumpkin show at the zoo second only to trick-or-treating as a holiday tradition.

Roger Williams Park Zoo
1000 Elmwood Ave., Providence, RI 02907
(401) 785-3510
rwpzoo.org

TIP
Ride the two-seat Soaring Eagle Zip Ride for a witch's-eye view of the glowing pumpkins from 115 feet high.

HIT THE BLOCK FOR SUMMER CONCERTS
AT BALLARD'S

Dancing with your toes in the sand is what summer is all about at Ballard's, a lively beach bar, concert venue, and hotel just steps away from the Block Island Ferry terminal. Tradition calls for ordering the first drink of the day on the ferry trip over from Point Judith—make it a surprisingly excellent Bloody Mary from the onboard bar—before staking your claim on Ballard's beach for a day of live country, rock, or reggae on summer weekends. You can bring coolers onto the beach but not your own alcohol; you'll pay a little extra at the Ballard's bar for beer and cocktails, but figure that as the price of admission, since there's no cover charge for the music.

Ballard's
42 Water St., New Shoreham, RI 02807
(401) 466-2231
ballardsbi.com

TIP
Take a break to hydrate and then sweat off some of those drinks with a game of beach volleyball—the Ballard's courts come with great views of the ocean and Old Harbor.

DO A DOUBLE FEATURE
AT THE DRIVE-IN

Back in the heyday of the drive-in movie, families would pile into station wagons (with maybe some neighborhood kids filling up the extra seats and "wayback") to catch a double feature for a few bucks per carload. SUVs have replaced the "family truckster," but otherwise the experience remains classic Americana at Smithfield's Rustic Tri View Drive-In. The last drive-in theater in Rhode Island has been around since the 1950s and even survived a stint of showing X-rated films in the seventies. Today, it's a family-friendly operation where you still pay one price for as many people as you can squeeze into the car, with a pair of first-run movies showing on three screens. The Rustic is open from April to September.

Rustic Tri View Drive-In
1195 Eddie Dowling Hwy., North Smithfield, RI 02896
(401) 484-5452
yourneighborhoodtheatre.com/location/7312/rustic-tri-view-drive-in

TIP

Unlike some other drive-ins—not to mention indoor movie theaters—you can bring your own snacks and drinks to the show. That said, ordering from the concession stand between the three screens is part of the fun, and the menu includes soft-serve ice cream and other treats you can't make at home.

TUNE IN TO LIVE MUSIC
AT THE GREENWICH ODEUM

Born as a vaudeville house and for many years operated as a movie theater, the Greenwich Odeum on East Greenwich's Main Street has returned to its roots as a venue for live performances. With just 410 seats, the Odeum is an intimate place to enjoy the music of touring acts like the Bacon Brothers, Blue Öyster Cult, and Ricky Lee Jones, as well as tribute bands, comedy shows, and big-screen revivals of classics like *The Godfather* and *Monty Python and the Holy Grail*. The downtown location is perfect for dinner and a show, and renovations over the last decade-plus have transformed the Odeum into a truly beautiful showplace. If one of your favorite bands is coming to town, this is the place to get up close and personal with your musical heroes.

Greenwich Odeum
59 Main St., East Greenwich, RI 02818
(401) 885-4000
greenwichodeum.com

TIP

For a pre-show drink, get your tiki on at
Kai Bar; for dinner, La Masseria has fine
Italian dining. MainStreet Coffee is great for
after-show coffee and also has a martini bar
known for its espresso-infused cocktails.

Narragansett surfing (Photo credit: John Woodmansee)

SPORTS AND RECREATION

SADDLE UP
FOR NEWPORT POLO

The summer polo series at Portsmouth's Glen Farm isn't only for rich swells—general admission is just fifteen dollars—but you can embrace your inner Gatsby by rolling up to the match with a bottle of something bubbly and some crudités and joining the tailgaters lining the polo grounds for a mid-summer soiree. Newport's annual international polo series has thundering ponies, spirited competition, and a touch of pomp and circumstance as Team USA/Newport takes on challengers from around the world. This being Newport, of course there are luxury boxes and VIP tents, but everyone joins in between "chukkas"—the seven-minute periods when mallet-wielding riders compete—to walk the field and tamp down the divots left by the galloping horses.

Newport International Polo Grounds & Pavilion at Glen Farm
250 Linden Ln., Portsmouth, RI 02871
(401) 846-0200
nptpolo.com

TIP
If your dreams canter toward learning to play the world's oldest team sport yourself, Newport Polo also offers polo lessons each summer.

SPOT A SNOWY OWL
AT SACHUEST POINT

Sachuest Point in Middletown is a popular stopover point for migratory birds, which can be found in the National Wildlife Refuge's salt marshes and shrubland and along the beaches below the short cliffs that ring the point. Harlequin ducks, sparrows, and the endangered piping plover are among the birds you can spot here, but the true feather in your cap would be to spy an elusive snowy owl. These majestic Arctic natives (Harry Potter fans may know that Hedwig, Harry's owl, is a snowy) have been seen in larger numbers in Rhode Island in recent years, and Sachuest Point is a good place to see one for a simple reason: they are skilled predators that feed on other birds residing in the park, especially ducks.

Sachuest Point National Wildlife Refuge
769 Sachuest Point Rd., Middletown, RI 02842
(401) 619-2680
fws.gov/refuge/sachuest_point

TIP
Unlike many owls, snowy owls are daytime hunters; that and their striking white plumage make them relatively easy to spot if they are around.

CATCH A GAME
AT CARDINES FIELD

Negro League star and Baseball Hall of Fame member Satchel Paige played here. So did Yogi Berra, Bob Feller, and—more recently—future major leaguers Stephen Strasburg, Andre Ethier, and former Newport Gulls catcher Chris Iannetta, who is now with the Colorado Rockies. A field of dreams in the heart of Newport, Cardines Field dates to 1908, making it older than Fenway Park or any other major league stadium. Within its green walls, both the Gulls of the New England Collegiate Baseball League and the teams of the George Donnelly Sunset League play games throughout the summer, often to stands full of families attracted by the Gulls' cheap tickets (five dollars or less) and frequent promotions. Fans of the "summer game" can spend hours basking in Cardines's small-town atmosphere and enjoy the high-quality play on the field for less than the cost of a beer at any Newport bar.

Cardines Field
20 America's Cup Ave., Newport, RI 02840
newportgulls.pointstreaksites.com/view/newportgulls

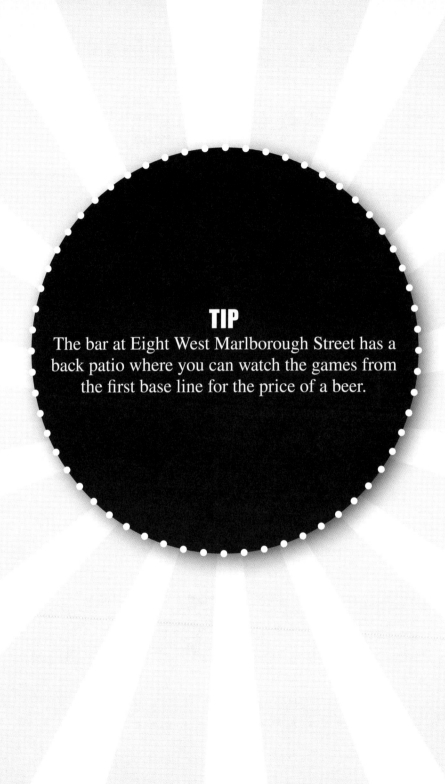

TIP

The bar at Eight West Marlborough Street has a back patio where you can watch the games from the first base line for the price of a beer.

GO SURFING
ON NARRAGANSETT BEACH

Narragansett Beach is an unexpected surfing mecca right here in Rhode Island. Not to be confused with Mavericks or the Banzai Pipeline, the town beach in Narragansett nonetheless attracts a regular crowd of hardcore East Coast surfers, who generally adhere to the credo "the worse the weather, the better the surfing." As a result, you're just as likely to see wetsuit-clad surfers here in the dead of winter as on a hot summer day. That said, there's always a good lineup along the seawall, and if you're a novice there are several options for getting your toes on a surfboard and hanging ten. Warm Winds Surf Shop is just a couple of blocks off the beach and offers individual and group lessons, as does the Narragansett Surf & Skate Shop.

Narragansett Town Beach
Boston Neck Rd., Narragansett, RI 02882
narragansettri.gov/323/narragansett-town-beach

TIP
If surfing seems a little too gnarly for you, take a stand-up paddle board lesson instead.

GALLOP IN THE SURF
ON BLOCK ISLAND

Fun fact about Block Island: you can actually walk on the beach around the entire island. Here's another: it's one of the only places in Rhode Island where you can ride a horse on the beach. Rustic Rides Farm is located on the quieter west side of the island and takes both newbies and experienced equestrians on one- and two-hour rides that include a trot along the beach as well as down quiet roads lined with stone walls and through a protected nature preserve. Veteran riders also have the opportunity to gallop through the sand and take their mounts right into the surf. Rides are available throughout the day, but for a truly memorable experience, book a sunset beach trot.

Rustic Rides Farm
1173 West Side Rd., New Shoreham, RI 02807
(401) 466-5060
facebook.com/rusticrideshorsefarm

TIP

If you didn't rent a bike or scooter, Rustic Rides offers free pickup service for guests with reservations.

TOUR THE EAST BAY
BY PEDAL POWER

Rhode Island has eight excellent off-road bike paths—that's a lot for a small state! The East Bay Bike Path, which runs from downtown Providence to the heart of Bristol, stands apart in a couple of ways: it was the first and it's also the most scenic. Built largely on the bed of the former Providence, Warren & Bristol Railroad, the rail-trail spends much of its length within sight of water as it passes through the coastal towns of East Providence, Barrington, Tiverton, Bristol, and Warren, including Narragansett Bay, the Providence River, the Warren River, the Barrington River, and Brickyard Pond. Downtown Bristol and Warren are short detours when it's time for lunch, shopping, or sightseeing. The route is mostly flat, but give yourself a pat on the back when you return to your starting point—you've just biked almost thirty miles through some of the most beautiful parts of Rhode Island.

dot.ri.gov/community/bikeri

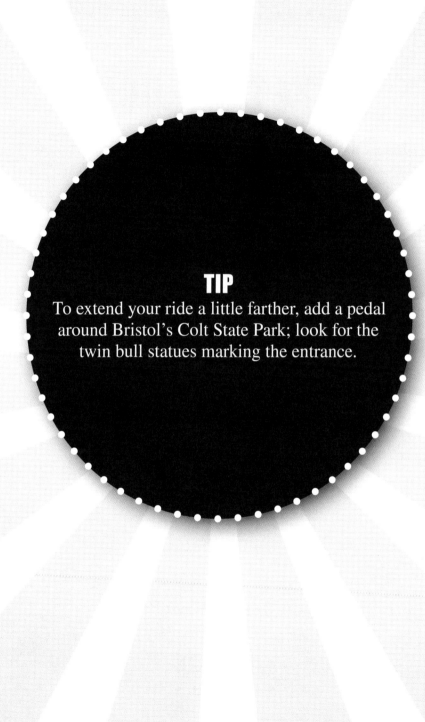

TIP

To extend your ride a little farther, add a pedal around Bristol's Colt State Park; look for the twin bull statues marking the entrance.

BIKE THE BLOCK

Block Island can be hillier and windier than you might imagine, but touring by bike is still the best way to see the island. You can bring your own bikes on the ferry (for a fee) or rent at Beach Rose Bicycles, and the Block Island Tourism Council has helpfully laid out a seven-and-a-half-mile loop trail that will get you to most of the island's major sites, including the Southeast Lighthouse, the Mohegan Bluffs, and Rodman's Hollow. If you're feeling more adventurous, you can add another eight and a half miles for the out-and-back to the North Lighthouse and the Great Salt Pond. Optional stops including hiking the trails through Nature Conservancy lands and visiting the island's historic cemetery, and there are plenty of choices along the way when it's time for a snack or drink, including Dead Eye Dick's bar and restaurant.

Beach Rose Bicycles
1622 Roslyn Ln., New Shoreham, RI 02807
(401) 466-5925
beachrosebicycles.com

TIP

Make time to visit the yak, alpacas, and other exotic animals at the Abrams Animal Farm behind the 1661 Inn and the Hotel Manisses.

PLAY KEEPER
AT THE ROSE ISLAND LIGHTHOUSE

The Rose Island Lighthouse in Newport Harbor is one of more than two dozen lighthouses in Rhode Island, but it's the only one where you can play keeper for a night. Built in 1870 and listed on the National Register of Historic Places, the lighthouse sits in the shadow of the Newport Bridge and can be visited on day trips or booked for overnight stays in the former lighthouse keeper's quarters, a pair of first-floor bedrooms, or the former foghorn and barracks buildings. Either way, it's an unforgettable experience, with guests getting most of the island for their private use during their stay as well as 360-degree vistas of Narragansett Bay. The lighthouse isn't entirely off the grid—there is electricity and ferry boats do occasionally drop by with visitors—but it is peaceful enough to lure the kids off their devices and into a kayak to explore, fish, take a swim, or sing a sea chantey around the fire pit.

Rose Island Lighthouse Foundation
(401) 847-4242
roseisland.org

TIP

If you cherish solitude, book a stay between November and May, when the lighthouse museum is closed, the ferry isn't running, and the odds are lower that other guests will be staying at the lighthouse.

GO KARTING
IN LINCOLN

Many of us have memories of puttering around on roadside go-kart tracks or—even worse—the painfully slow version of karting found at amusement parks. R1 Indoor Karting is a whole other experience: you'll feel like a real race car driver behind the wheel of these electric go-karts, which have a top speed of forty miles per hour. Not much in a car, maybe, but in karting that's blazing fast, meaning you'll whip around the turns of R1's indoor, one-third-of-a-mile-long Mega Track. The experience is fun, but edgy: each race is seven laps, and drivers compete not only against each other but the clock. There's no champagne splash for the winner, but you can toast your efforts after the checkered flag at the trackside Fuel restaurant and sports bar.

R1 Indoor Karting
100 Higginson Ave., Lincoln, RI 02865
(401) 721-5554
r1indoorkarting.com

TIP
Buying three races for sixty dollars is a better deal than one for twenty-five dollars—and you'll want to go more than once.

DIVE WITH SHARKS
OFF THE RHODE ISLAND COAST

You can sink your teeth into some real adventure with Capt. Charlie Donilon, who owns the fishing and diving boat *Snappa* and is the one and only charter captain in Rhode Island who takes people diving with sharks. *Jaws*, you may recall, was set in New England, and while you're not likely to see any great whites, the local waters are full of big sharks—makos, blues, and basking sharks, to name a few. The sharks live in the deep ocean, so Capt. Donilon will take you up to fifty miles out before lowering you in a cage into chummed waters swarming with sharks. Up to three people can go into the cage at once—that's either reassuring company or more items on the buffet, depending on your perspective. (Don't worry, you'll be perfectly safe in the anti-shark cage, which only goes about eight feet underwater.)

Snappa Charters
2 Congdon Dr., Wakefield, RI 02879
(401) 487-9044
snappacharters.com

TIP
If the shark cage seems too intense, you can also see the sharks from a special viewing platform on the surface.

GREET THE DAY
AT BEAVERTAIL STATE PARK

The southern tip of Conanicut (Jamestown) Island has been treasured for its commanding views of Narragansett Bay since Colonial times, when both a lighthouse and fort were built here to protect the bay and those who sailed it. The Beavertail Lighthouse still stands—the current tower dates to 1856—and Beavertail State Park remains the most dramatic place in Rhode Island to get an unobstructed view of the sun rising over the Atlantic. You'll hear the awesome power of nature as the ocean waves slam against the rocks beneath the lighthouse before you can see the pounding surf in the first light of dawn. Soak in the moment before giving the local fishermen a friendly wave and getting on with your day.

Beavertail State Park
Beavertail Rd., Jamestown, RI 02835
(401) 884-2010
riparks.com/locations/locationbeavertail.html

TIP
Warm up afterwards at Jamestown's Slice of Heaven bakery and café, which serves breakfast, lunch, and fresh-baked cakes, cookies, and other sweet and savory treats.

SEE THE SEALS
OF NARRAGANSETT BAY

Harbor seals have long made their home on the rocky outcroppings and beaches of Narragansett Bay, and it's always a thrill to see these big marine mammals in their natural habitat rather than in an aquarium. Spotting a seal is easy enough if you know where to look—they can grow up to six feet long and weigh 350 pounds. From land, perhaps the best vantage point is from the beach at Rome Point in North Kingstown, since a population of harbor seals has made rocks just offshore more or less a permanent winter home. You also can see seals when they occasionally haul up on Rhode Island's beaches, but the best bet for a close-up view is to join Save the Bay—a local nonprofit dedicated to preserving Rhode Island's aquatic environment—on a Seal Watch Tour by boat out of Newport Harbor.

Save the Bay
(401) 203-SEAL (7325)
savebay.org

TIP
Seals actually blend in pretty well with the grayish rocks of Narragansett Bay, so bring along some binoculars for the best views.

ROUND UP A GLASS ORB
ON BLOCK ISLAND

Every year, glassblowing artist Eben Horton of Wakefield hides more than five hundred hand-blown glass orbs around Block Island—his way of giving back to a place he loves as well as raising awareness about conservation projects on the island. Making a summer hike into a treasure hunt has been a tradition for locals and visitors alike since Horton launched the Glass Float Project about a decade ago; finding one of the clear-glass balls hidden on the beaches and along the Greenway trails maintained by the Nature Conservancy is a thrill. It's finders-keepers for these priceless memories, which are individually numbered and distributed every summer. If you're really lucky, you may find one of a handful of special balls created by Horton each year, such as an orb covered entirely in gold leaf.

Glass Station
446 Main St., South Kingstown, RI 02879
(401) 788-2500
glassfloatproject.com

TIP

If your search is unsuccessful, you can always stop at the Glass Station in Wakefield and buy one of Horton's beautiful glass orbs or other glassware.

GET RUGGED
ON THE NEWPORT CLIFF WALK

Apart from going to the beach, walking the historic Cliff Walk is probably the most popular outdoor activity in Newport. But while a lot of people have "done" the Cliff Walk, few traverse the entire path running behind Newport's famous mansions and along the cliffs overlooking Easton's Beach. The first two-thirds of the three-and-a-half-mile trail is paved and, as they might have said during the Gilded Age, quite civilized. The last section, however, is a dirt trail over rugged and rocky terrain. Most visitors just walk for an hour or so before turning around, but you'll get a real sense of adventure (and accomplishment) if you do the entire two-and-a-half-hour walk. You'll also earn access to Belmont Beach—a local surfer's mecca—and Reject's (Third) Beach, the private strand normally reserved for Newport's blue bloods.

cliffwalk.com

TIP
Begin and end your cliff walk loop at Memorial Boulevard so you can celebrate in style with drinks or a meal at the elegant Chanler at Cliff Walk hotel.

PREPARE FOR AWE
ON THE TRESTLE TRAIL

Rhode Island is generally a pretty flat place, so dramatic vistas tend to be a little lacking. One exception can be found along Coventry's Trestle Trail, a hiking, biking, and walking trail that's now part of the Washington Secondary Bike Path. Follow the state's longest bike path (nineteen miles) about as far west toward Connecticut as you can, and you'll discover how the Trestle Trail got its name: you'll cross a river on a high-altitude bridge built for the former Providence, Hartford, and Fishkill Railroad. It's one of the most beautiful and unexpectedly dramatic spots in the state and well worth the steady uphill pedal to get there (of course your return trip will be all downhill!).

dot.ri.gov/community/bikeri/washington.php

TIP
Riding the Washington Secondary Bike Path from end to end is Rhode Island in microcosm, starting from the east end in urban Cranston, passing the mills that powered the Industrial Revolution, then becoming increasingly green and peaceful as you head into the rural western half of the state.

BEACH IT
AT THE MOHEGAN BLUFFS

You have to earn your place on the beach at the Mohegan Bluffs: the two-hundred-foot clay cliffs on the southeast end of Block Island are accessible only by climbing a 141-step staircase (so don't forget your sunscreen in the car). Once you're down, however, the views of the cliffs and the sea are equally magnificent. The product of steady erosion by the storms and surf of the Atlantic Ocean, the bluffs get their name from a legendary battle where the native Manissean tribe drove a raiding party of Mohegans from the mainland over the edge and to their deaths. There are other fine beaches on Block Island that are easier to reach, but this is the one to come to if you cherish solitude—the climb tends to keep the crowds smaller even in the height of summer.

Mohegan Bluffs
blockislandinfo.com/island-events/mohegan-bluffs

TIP

Combine your visit to the Mohegan Bluffs with a stop at the nearby Southeast Light, a sixty-seven-foot-high lighthouse built in 1875.

SCOPE OUT SOME STARS
AT NINIGRET PARK

Ninigret Park, a former Naval Air Station in Charlestown, is one of the darkest spots between New York and Boston; not coincidentally, there's a powerful telescope in the park that's open to the public for stargazing every Friday night and on special occasions like meteor showers, eclipses, and the rare passing of comets. On a clear, moonless night, there's no better place to view the planets, stars, and galaxies than the Frosty Drew Observatory, which is equipped with a powerful Meade Schmidt Cassegrain LX200 sixteen-inch telescope, as well as several other telescopes, including those lugged to the park by amateur astronomers, who are usually generous and excited about sharing the views through their own equipment.

Ninigret State Park
61-62 Park Ln., Ninigret Park, Charlestown, RI 02813
(401) 859-1450
frostydrew.org

TIP

Come prepared with warm layers in the winter and long pants in the warmer months. Bundling up against cold nights (when visibility tends to be best) or the summer mosquitoes is a small price to pay for nature's greatest light show.

CHART A COURSE
FOR PRUDENCE ISLAND

For a small state, Rhode Island retains a lot of open space, and that's true of the islands of Narragansett Bay too. Smack in the center of the bay is Prudence Island, the state's fourth-largest island but with a fraction of the population of Newport, Jamestown, and Block Island. In fact, fewer than one hundred people live on Prudence Island year-round, and deer easily outnumber the human residents in the off-season. A ferry that runs daily from downtown Bristol can get you to Prudence Island in about half an hour, but if you go, you'll still be one of the few outsiders to visit. Frankly, there's not much to see: no restaurants or hotels, and but a single store—but you can spend a relaxed day hiking or pedaling to sights like the Sandy Point Lighthouse, Farnham Farm, and the one-room schoolhouse; swimming on the local beaches; and hiking the conservation lands that cover most of the island.

Prudence Island Ferry
147 Thames St., Bristol, RI 02809
(401) 683-0430
prudencebayislandstransport.com

TIP
If you want to pedal around Prudence Island, bring a mountain bike. If you plan to hike, be sure to protect yourself against the unfortunately large local population of disease-carrying deer ticks.

ROAR WITH THE CROWD
AT A PROVIDENCE BRUINS GAME

Hockey passion runs high in Rhode Island, where many people have French Canadian roots and grew up with the game, and passion runs high for the Boston Bruins and the Providence College hockey teams in particular. The state also gives a lot of love to its resident minor league team, the Providence Bruins, part of the American Hockey League and a training ground for players dreaming of playing in the NHL. Games are usually on Friday nights and Sunday afternoons, and for a ticket that usually costs less than twenty dollars you'll get a big-league entertainment experience at Dunkin' Donuts Center. Expect a high level of play and plenty of passion both on ice and off as up-and-coming players battle for attention in Boston and established stars work their way back from injuries or look to restart their careers.

Providence Bruins
1 La Salle Square, Providence, RI 02903
providencebruins.com

TIP

Hold off on making a drink or bathroom run between periods so you don't miss the always entertaining peewee games that start right after the P-Bruins clear the ice.

TAKE A SNOWY SLIDE
AT YAWGOO VALLEY SKI AREA

Rhode Island has a lot going for it—beaches, bay, forests, big city, small towns. One thing it lacks, however, is anything even resembling a mountain. Yet Yawgoo Valley, Rhode Island's only ski area, manages to eke every last thrill possible out of its 245 vertical feet, with a pair of chairlifts serving about a dozen trails, plus a popular tubing park that draws big family crowds. Both day and night skiing are available, and while nobody will mistake Yawgoo for Vail or Aspen, it's a great place to take a bunch of short but fast runs, learn to ski or snowboard, and generally to spend a few hours playing in the snow before retiring back to The Max for a beer or two.

Yawgoo Valley Ski Area
160 Yawgoo Valley Rd., Exeter, RI 02822
(401) 294-3802
yawgoo.com

TIP
Ticket sales are capped for both the ski hill and tubing, so buy in advance (especially for tubing) so you don't get shut out.

SCIALO BROS. BAKERY (page 8)
Photo credit: Bob Curley

CRESCENT PARK
LOOFF
CAROUSEL

CIRCA
1895

OCEAN MIST (page 40)
Photo credit: Bob Curley

SECOND BEACH
Photo credit: Discover Newport

GASPEE DAYS (page 128)
Photo credit: Bob Curley

SLATER MILL (page 152)
Photo credit: RI Commerc Corporation

PROVIDENCE RINK (page 128)
Photo credit: Bob Curley

WICKFORD HARBOR
Photo credit: Bob Curley

PERRY RASO, MATUNUCK OYSTER BAR (page 36)
Photo credit: Grace Lentini

GILBERT STUART BIRTHPLACE AND MUSEUM (page 101)
Photo credit: Bob Curley

SKYDIVE
OVER NEWPORT

Let's face it, skydiving is a bucket-list item for a lot of people regardless of where they live—there's nothing specific to Rhode Island about it. That said, skydiving over Newport is a particularly spectacular experience thanks to the views of Narragansett Bay and distant points of interest like Martha's Vineyard and Block Island as you plunge toward earth at 120 miles per hour. Skydive Newport only does tandem jumps, meaning you'll be strapped into your parachute with an expert instructor on your back. If you're a first-timer—and you probably are if this is a life goal for you—tandem is really the only way to go anyway. Both takeoff and drop zones are located in Middletown, only a short drive from downtown Newport.

Skydive Newport
211 Airport Access Rd., Middletown, RI 02842
(401) 845-0393
skydivenewport.com

TIP
Toast your successful landing at nearby Newport Vineyards, where locally grown grapes are turned into a variety of wines and there's also a brewery and the excellent Brix restaurant to enjoy.

KAYAK
THE NARROW RIVER

Ride the tide for a leisurely paddle up and down the Pettaquamscutt (Narrow) River, which runs from Carr Pond in North Kingstown to the Atlantic Ocean in Narragansett. You can bring your own boat or rent from Narrow River Kayaks on Middlebridge Road for a day-long adventure that can include paddling to ocean and river beaches, through ponds and lakes, drifting along shores lined with beautiful homes, or venturing into the ocean waves or the undeveloped wetlands of the John H. Chafee National Wildlife Refuge. Whether you are kayaking or standup paddleboarding, the keys to a fun day on the river include packing plenty of water, something for lunch, and sunscreen, and, especially, checking the tide charts so that you can ride the incoming and outgoing tides, not fight against them.

Narrow River Kayaks
94 Middlebridge Rd., Narragansett, RI 02882
(401) 789-0334
narrowriverkayaks.com

TIP

The Narrow River Preservation Association publishes paddling maps for the upper and lower sections of the river; an upper river trip can be combined with a visit to the Gilbert Stuart Birthplace and Museum, home of the artist whose likeness of George Washington appears on the one-dollar bill.

SKATE
IN KENNEDY PLAZA

The historic and modern buildings of downtown Providence rise up around the Providence Rink in Kennedy Plaza, including City Hall and the historic Biltmore hotel, recently rechristened as the stylish Graduate. It's a beautiful backdrop to an afternoon or evening of gliding across the ice on skates or, for a competitive change of pace, get behind the wheel for a clash of on-ice bumper cars. The ice rink is frozen between November and March, but the bumper cars also operate during the summer, when the rink switches over to Astroturf for activities like bubble soccer and human bowling. Part of the Alex and Ani City Center, the rink is open daily from 10 a.m. to 10 p.m.

Alex and Ani City Center
2 Kennedy Plaza, Providence, RI 02903
(401) 680-7390
theprovidencerink.com

TIP
The rink and heated pavilion can also be rented before or after regular business hours for hockey games or private events.

STEP OUT
TO RHODE ISLAND'S BEST WATERFALL

The highest point in Rhode Island is just 812 feet above sea level, so it's not a landscape that's favorable to dramatic waterfalls tumbling over high cliffs. In fact, nearly every waterfall in Rhode Island was created by damming a river during the Industrial Revolution. The exception is Stepstone Falls in West Greenwich, a natural series of cascades where the Wood River tumbles across flat and wide granite ledges. More scenic than tall, the waterfall drops just ten feet over a one-hundred-foot length of river. But visiting is easy—it's just a few hundred feet off the aptly named Falls River Road—and you can also reach Stepstone Falls by hiking the Ben Utter Trail, which traces the path of the Wood River for 3.4 miles in Exeter and West Greenwich.

Stepstone Falls
alltrails.com/trail/us/rhode-island/stepstone-falls-via-ben-utter-trail
or
newenglandwaterfalls.com/ri-stepstonefalls.html

TIP
Stepstone Falls can get pretty wild after a rainstorm; spring is often the best time to visit thanks to higher water levels.

FISH FOR STRIPERS
ON NARRAGANSETT BAY

Striped bass are big, powerful predators that chase prey like menhaden into Narragansett Bay each spring, and they're also the most sought-after fish among anglers who head out into the local waters on boats or cast a line from docks and bridges over the bay. A striper will give you a good fight, but it's worth the effort: a legal (twenty-eight inches long or more) catch will give you some tasty fillets and a good story to tell your friends. Striper fishing is part of Rhode Island culture, and there are multiple charter boats that will take you out on the bay for a morning or afternoon of fishing, such as Flippin Out Fishing Charters of Portsmouth. You'll get to keep one striper per day, but you can also fish for bluefish, black sea bass, and tautog in Narragansett Bay, which local fishermen say is cleaner and more full of fish than it has been in decades.

Flippin Out Fishing Charters
50 Mail Coach Rd., Portsmouth, RI 02871
(401) 529-2267
flippinoutcharters.com

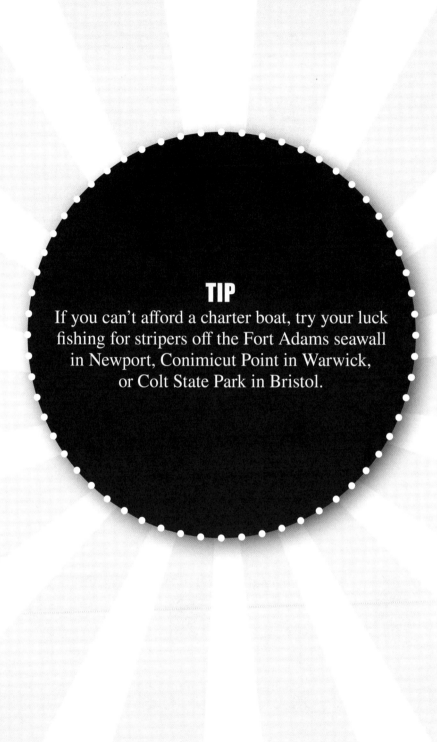

TIP

If you can't afford a charter boat, try your luck fishing for stripers off the Fort Adams seawall in Newport, Conimicut Point in Warwick, or Colt State Park in Bristol.

PLAY AND STAY
AT THE MAXWELL MAYS PRESERVE

Famed Rhode Island artist Maxwell Mays donated his three-hundred-acre property and lakeside cottage in Coventry to the Audubon Society of Rhode Island upon his death in 2009. The land and eleven-acre Carr Pond became the Maxwell Mays Wildlife Refuge, and Audubon now rents the two-bedroom cottage to overnight guests, who can enjoy the seclusion of having the park to themselves from dusk to dawn. The charming cottage has a fireplace, outdoor grill, screened porch, and spacious deck overlooking Maxwell Mays Pond and sleeps up to five guests. Overnight visitors can fish and make use of the canoe and kayak that come with the cottage or hike the refuge's five miles of trails, which include a self-guided nature trail.

Maxwell Mays Preserve
2082 Victory Hwy., Coventry, RI 02816
asri.org/services/mays-lakehouse.html

TIP
Visitors are told to bring their own linens, towels, food, and water, so be sure to pack well if you go.

CLIMB
NEUTACONKANUT HILL

Neutaconkanut is a hill with a history: the "Great Hill" marked the boundary of the original land grant made by the Narragansett tribe to Rhode Island founder Roger Williams, and it stands as the highest point in Providence. As the city grew dense at its feet, the eighty-eight-acre hill was almost miraculously preserved, with hiking trails snaking through the woodlands on its sides and peak and a former ski slope that is popular for winter sledding. Restored trails originally cut in the 1930s lead to the summit, with its unobstructed views of downtown Providence, and along the way you'll find a variety of wildlife, including deer and fox living in the oak and hickory forest rising above the crowded streets of Olneyville.

675 Plainfield St., Providence, RI 02909
(401) 649-4366
nhill.org

TIP
The Neutaconkanut Hill Conservancy leads periodic guided hikes in the park.

JOIN A SUMMER FLOAT PARTY
ON NARRAGANSETT BAY

Getting into a boat on the bay is fun almost anytime, but when you pull alongside dozens of other boats and add some floats, music, and libations, that's an unforgettable day on the water. Newport Harbor is the hot spot for summer float parties, which can be defined simply as two or more boats spontaneously tying up together and sharing drinks and laughs. They're especially popular during the weekends of the Newport Folk and Jazz Festivals, where you'll find scores of boats anchored offshore from Fort Adams to enjoy the music from a distant, but free, vantage point. Then there's Aquapalooza, a big annual gathering of the fleet held in July in the waters of Potter's Cove off Prudence Island that includes live music with a float area set up in front of the stage for watching the show.

TIP
You'll need a boat—or a friend with one—to join a float party, including Aquapalooza.

LEARN TO JIB AND TACK
AT SAIL NEWPORT

Rhode Island is the Ocean State—fully one-third of the entire state is water, not land. So if you don't know how to sail, you're really missing out on a lot of what the state has to offer. Sail Newport, a nonprofit organization located at Fort Adams, offers sailing lessons for beginners as well as old salts. Newbies can learn the basics on the school's fleet of easy-to-handle J/22 and Rhodes 19 sailboats, and the boats are also available for rental, so you can practice your newfound skills anytime. Once you've got the basics down, you can take part in the school's weeknight fleet racing program, with the course set up between Rose and Goat Islands in Narragansett Bay.

Sail Newport
72 Fort Adams Dr., Newport, RI 02840
(401) 846-1983
sailnewport.org

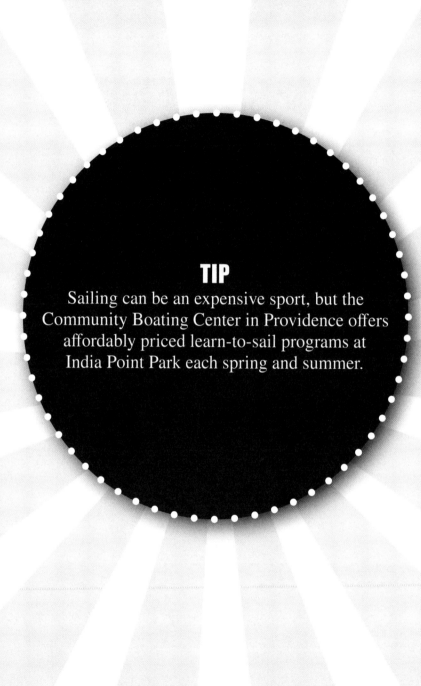

TIP

Sailing can be an expensive sport, but the Community Boating Center in Providence offers affordably priced learn-to-sail programs at India Point Park each spring and summer.

CAMP ON THE SAND
AT EAST BEACH

East Beach is not only one of the most isolated stretches of shoreline in Rhode Island, but it's also one of a handful of beaches on the East Coast that allow you to drive your car onto the sand. Accessible from East Beach Road in Charlestown, East Beach runs for three miles along the southern edge of Ninigret Pond before dead-ending at the Charlestown Breachway. With a required permit in hand you can take your Jeep or other four-wheel-drive vehicle onto the East Beach Sand Trail, which in turn offers access to the beach and a pair of campgrounds, each with ten primitive campsites. Only thirty cars are permitted on East Beach each day, so odds are good that you'll find a stretch of sand all to yourself, especially once the sun sets.

East Beach
East Beach Rd., Charlestown, RI 02813
rhodeislandstateparks.reserveamerica.com

TIP
East Beach driving is limited to the Sand Trail in the summer, but come in the off-season (September 15–April 1) and you can take your 4x4 right to the water's edge.

FLY A KITE
AT BRENTON POINT

Located at the spot where Narragansett Bay meets the Atlantic Ocean, Brenton Point State Park in Newport is known for its steady ocean breezes, making it the perfect spot to send a kite soaring above the fancy homes of Ocean Drive. Any weekend from spring to fall you'll find people hoisting kites of all shapes and sizes at Brenton Point, from flying fish to graceful dragons. But the really spectacular kites come out during the annual Newport Kite Festival in July, including seemingly life-sized whale kites, lobsters, and squadrons of flying aliens. If you don't have a kite at home, Kitt Kites sells them right at Brenton Point from April to October, or you can get one at the Magic Studio on Thames Street in downtown Newport.

Brenton Point State Park
Ocean Dr., Newport, RI 02840
(401) 849-4562
riparks.com/locations/locationbrentonpoint.html

TIP
The eighty-three-acre park, which occupies the grounds of an estate called The Bells, is also great for picnicking and hiking, including to the decaying ruins of a former carriage house and a still-open stone observation tower.

TAKE THE WATERS
AT THE BODHI SPA

I've never said no to a massage, and while facials and wraps aren't really my thing, I generally love spas. The Water Journey at Newport's Bodhi Spa is a little bit different: it's not all about pampering, but rather is a form of hydrotherapy that's said to improve circulation and remove toxins from the body. The seven-stage journey begins with a dip in a warm Dead Sea salt pool, followed by a spell in the steam room; from there, you alternate between soothing stops in the sauna and a 104-degree salt pool with brief but invigorating plunges into a fifty-degree cold pool. The latter is hard to take for the recommended one minute, but the end result is a feeling of both enhanced wellness and accomplishment, which you can get over and over again by repeating the water course during your visit, which has no set time limit.

Bodhi Spa
654 Thames St., Newport, RI 02840
(401) 619-4916
thebodhispa.com

TIP

Missing out on that massage? The spa offers a full menu of traditional treatments, and you'll get half off the Water Journey if you book any other spa service.

NET SOME GREAT TENNIS ACTION
AT THE NEWPORT HALL OF FAME TOURNAMENT

I've been to big tennis tournaments like the U.S. Open, Indian Wells, and the Miami Open, but some of my greatest tennis memories have been at the Newport Tennis Hall of Fame's annual grass court tournament. Walking onto the grounds of the shingle-style, Charles McKim-designed Newport Casino feels like entering a shrine, but despite its grand-sounding name and Newport address, the July tournament (held shortly after Wimbledon) is remarkably laid back and intimate. Over here, you might see Lleyton Hewitt warming up on a side court; over there, American pros Sam Querrey and John Isner are hitting rocket shots on center court. Between matches, take the time to tour the Hall itself, full of memorabilia and interactive exhibits documenting the history of the game from its inception through the Open Era.

Newport Tennis Hall of Fame
194 Bellevue Ave., Newport, RI 02840
(401) 849-3990
tennisfame.com

TIP

If you're a true tennis junkie, get tickets for the Hall of Fame enshrinement ceremony held during the tournament, when new inductees are welcomed into the company of tennis legends like Laver, Borg, Billy Jean, and Navratilova.

SAIL A 12 METRE YACHT
IN NEWPORT HARBOR

Newport was the home base of arguably the most famous racing sailor in American history: Dennis Conner, four-time winner of the America's Cup 12 Metre yachting championship. Alas, the America's Cup was stolen away by the Aussies and hasn't returned, but yachting remains a rich tradition in Newport, and the unmistakable 12 Metre yachts still ply the local waters. Companies like 12 Meter Charters and America's Cup Charters offer leisurely two-hour sails in Newport Harbor and Narragansett Bay aboard past America's Cup winners like the *Columbia* (1958) and the *Weatherly* (1962), but you can up the thrill component considerably by joining a three-hour racing cruise (these boats were built for speed, after all) or chartering a yacht for a day of hands-on sailing.

12metercharters.com
americascupcharters.com

TIP
Wear some rain gear: you're almost certain to get wet no matter which cruise you choose!

GO QUAHOGGING
AND RAKE IN YOUR DINNER

The quahog—pronounced "ko-hog"—is the fat clam native to Rhode Island waters and found in the state's famous clam cakes, chowder, and "stuffies," or stuffed clams. Abundant in the shallow waters of Narragansett Bay and the state's coastal ponds, quahogs have been harvested by hand for millennia, as prehistoric shell middens (piles of discarded clamshells left by Native Americans) attest. Rhode Islanders can still be found quahogging all along the state's ample shoreline; you can technically dig clams by hand, but a good clam rake makes the job a lot easier. Popular quahogging spots include Ninigret Pond in Charlestown, Point Judith Pond in Narragansett, Conimicut Point in Warwick, and Colt State Park in Bristol. It's a bit of work, but it comes with a tasty reward that's quintessentially Rhode Island.

TIP
Check with the state Department of Environmental Regulation to ensure that the area you want to clam is open for quahogging, and if you're a non-resident you'll need to get a shellfishing permit first.

Rhythm & Roots Festival
(Photo credit: John Woodmansee)

CULTURE AND HISTORY

STOCK UP ON MUSICALS
AT THEATRE BY THE SEA

Summer stock theater has a rich history in coastal New England, and Theatre By The Sea continues a tradition of producing crowd-pleasing plays that began in 1933, mounting productions in the same shingled barn used since day one. Listed on the National Register of Historic Places, the rustic, five-hundred-seat theater about a mile from Matunuck Beach has alumni that include Groucho Marx and Marlon Brando. More recently, the theater has been staging four plays each summer, typically familiar musicals like *Mamma Mia!* and *Chicago*. The attached Bistro by the Sea is likewise open seasonally (May–September) and serves fresh local seafood—the perfect spot for a pre-show meal. After the curtain drops, you'll find many of the same actors taking part in a late-night cabaret show that's also open to the public.

Theatre By The Sea
364 Cards Pond Rd., Wakefield, RI 02879
(401) 782-8587
theatrebythesea.com

TIP
It's summer, so rather than waiting out intermission in your seat, order a cocktail and take it outside to the gazebo until the lights start flashing for the second act.

CONNECT WITH CULTURE
AT THE PROVIDENCE ART CLUB

There's both a public and a private side to the Providence Art Club; if you're in the know, you can experience both. Founded in 1880, the art club—the second oldest in America—occupies several historic buildings along Providence's Thomas Street, including the landmark Fleur de Lys Building, a Norman-style half-timbered former home built in 1885. Three galleries exhibiting club members' work are open to the public, which is a free opportunity not only to view the paintings and sculptures but also to admire the four historic buildings they're in. The art club also has a beautiful dining room in the 1790 Obadiah Brown House that's only open to members and their guests: silhouettes of former members look on approvingly as you enjoy lunch or the regular themed dinners held in the café and Founders Room.

Providence Art Club
11 Thomas St., Providence, RI 02903
(401) 331-1114
providenceartclub.org

TIP
Becoming a member is a bit of an investment for the casual art lover, so the real score is to get invited to dine with someone who's already in the club. Since everyone knows everyone in Rhode Island, it's best just to ask around!

LIGHT UP THE NIGHT
AT *WATERFIRE*

WaterFire might be the ultimate bucket-list event in Rhode Island. You'd be hard-pressed to find a Rhode Islander who hasn't attended at least one performance since this living music-fire-water "sculpture" was first staged by artist Barnaby Evans in 1994. *WaterFire* is usually the first thing locals recommend to first-time visitors, and attending never gets old no matter how many times you venture into Providence to experience the wood braziers burning on the downtown rivers, the haunting music echoing among the high-rise buildings, and the vision of boats full of black-clad docents feeding the flames. *WaterFire* can be enjoyed from the paths of the Providence Riverwalk or the amphitheater of Waterplace Park, but the most immersive way is to get on the water with La Gondola Providence or the Providence River Boat Company. Better yet, volunteer as a member of a wood-boat crew and you'll have a hand in keeping the fires burning yourself.

WaterFire Providence
475 Valley St., Providence, RI 02908
(401) 273-1155
waterfire.org

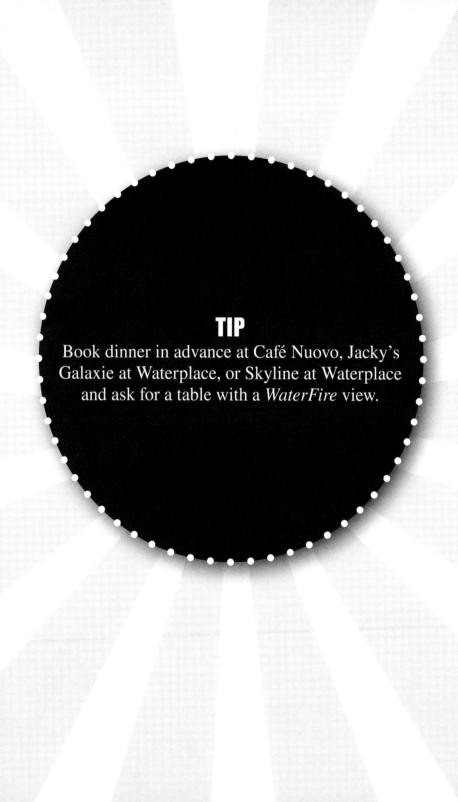

TIP

Book dinner in advance at Café Nuovo, Jacky's Galaxie at Waterplace, or Skyline at Waterplace and ask for a table with a *WaterFire* view.

HAVE A GARDEN PARTY
AT BLITHEWOLD

Here's some more of those weird Rhode Island facts: the smallest state is home to the tallest redwood tree east of the Rocky Mountains and the loftiest giant sequoia on the East Coast. Both of these monster trees are lovingly tended at Bristol's Blithewold, a thirty-three-acre estate where you can tour the arboretum, specialized gardens, and a forty-five-room mansion built on the coast of Narragansett Bay in 1906. Bamboo will grow almost anywhere, but Blithewold's dense Bamboo Grove is especially impressive, with stalks rising far overhead. The Rose Garden dates back to the early 1900s and includes a romantic moon gate, and there's also a beautiful tree-lined Lovers' Lane leading down to the shore of the bay—no wonder that Blithewold has been the site of thousands of weddings over the years.

Blithewold
101 Ferry Rd. (Rte. 114), Bristol, RI 02809
(401) 253-2707
blithewold.org

TIP
Blithewold is open year-round, but springtime—when more than fifty thousand daffodils are in bloom in and around the French-style bosquet during April and May—is especially spectacular.

GET FESTIVE
AT RHYTHM & ROOTS

A live music festival with Creole in its soul, Rhythm & Roots is an old-school gathering of the tribes held Labor Day weekend in Charlestown's Ninigret Park. The Newport Jazz and Folk Festivals have grown into big business over the decades, but Rhythm & Roots still feels like family, whether because of the familiar faces onstage (like the Knickerbocker All-Stars), the campers who make the park their home for the weekend, or the folks who set up mini encampments with flags flying—yet still let you fill their unoccupied seats when they're off at the concession stand or the craft market. The two-day festival channels New Orleans with a variety of Cajun and Creole acts, but you can also line-dance to country bands, chill out to folk music, or dance along to some good old-fashioned rock and roll and R&B.

Ninigret Park
4890A Old Post Rd., Charlestown, RI 02813
rhythmandroots.com

TIP
Bring a bathing suit so you can cool off between sets in the park's freshwater swimming pond, which even has a sandy beach and lifeguards on duty.

TOAST A PATRIOT
AT GASPEE DAYS IN PAWTUXET

Was the Boston Tea Party the most overrated act of rebellion in the American Revolution? Dressing up as Native Americans and tossing tea into Boston Harbor sounds fun and all, but unruly Rhode Islanders undertook a much more serious act of rebellion against King George more than a year earlier. Angered by Great Britain's enforcement of customs laws and the Stamp Act, local members of the Sons of Liberty saw their chance to strike a blow for freedom when the British revenue schooner HMS *Gaspee* ran aground off the coast of Warwick in Narragansett Bay. A raiding party boarded the ship, seized the captain and crew at gunpoint, looted the cargo, and burned the *Gaspee* to the waterline. Largely forgotten by history, the burning of the *Gaspee* is celebrated locally each June during Gaspee Days, which includes a parade featuring costumed militia groups, a colonial encampment, and a ceremonial torching of a *Gaspee* replica in the waters off the village of Pawtuxet.

gaspee.com

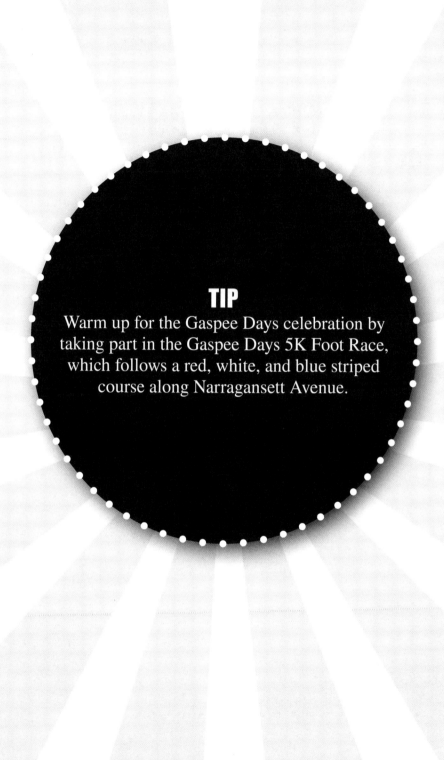

TIP

Warm up for the Gaspee Days celebration by taking part in the Gaspee Days 5K Foot Race, which follows a red, white, and blue striped course along Narragansett Avenue.

GET SCROOGED
AT TRINITY REP'S *A CHRISTMAS CAROL*

Providence's Trinity Repertory Company has been performing Charles Dickens's *A Christmas Carol* for decades, yet it manages to keep this classic morality play fresh and original from season to season. The hottest ticket in Rhode Island, Trinity Rep's annual Christmas play runs from Thanksgiving to the last week of December, and there may be no higher honor in the state's theater community than being chosen to play Scrooge. Some years the direction emphasizes the play's comic elements, other years, it's darker (such as the season a giant puppet depicted Death as the Ghost of Christmas Yet to Come). But it's always entertaining and always concludes with an uplifting message about charity, kindness, and redemption. What's more Christmas-y than that?

Trinity Repertory Company
201 Washington St., Providence, RI 02903
(401) 351-4242
trinityrep.com

TIP

Make reservations at Bravo Brasserie for a post-show meal and you might just run into Scrooge himself (or herself) as you toast the holiday season.

HAVE AN ANCIENT AND HORRIBLE DAY
IN CHEPACHET

Can Trump or Hillary lovers take a joke? They'd best be able to at the annual Ancients and Horribles Parade, held in Chepachet on the Fourth of July. Born as a mocking tribute to the formal "Ancients and Honorables" parades popular in the nineteenth and early twentieth centuries, the Chepachet parade has been making fun of politicians and other public figures since its founding in 1926. Floats and costumed marchers take aim at every sacred cow they can in a procession that turns the notion of the taciturn New Englander on its head. If you're easily offended, this probably isn't the parade for you; but if you take your First Amendment rights with a sense of humor, then you'll appreciate the sight of a truck full of manure "honoring" politicians or a Dick Cheney Hunting School float.

Ancients and Horribles Parade
Glocester Town Hall, 1145 Putnam Pike, PO Box B, Chepachet, RI 02814
(401) 568-6206
glocesterri.org/parade.htm

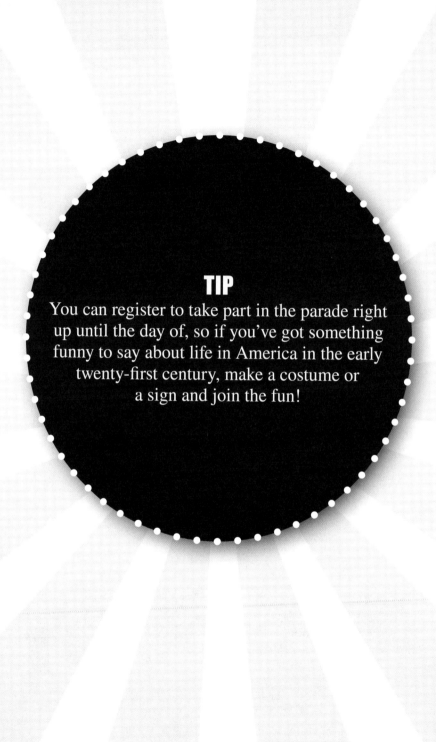

TIP

You can register to take part in the parade right up until the day of, so if you've got something funny to say about life in America in the early twenty-first century, make a costume or a sign and join the fun!

MEET
THE GREEN ANIMALS

Pruning bushes into the shapes of animals is something of a lost art—most of us are happy if we just keep the hedges in our yard trimmed. Countless kids (myself included) were first introduced to topiary gardens at Walt Disney World, where topiaries include characters like Mickey Mouse and Goofy and can be seen from the monorail and in Epcot. The oldest topiary garden in America, however, is right here in Portsmouth. Stroll through the Green Animals Topiary Garden, located on the former estate of nineteenth-century cotton magnate Thomas E. Brayton, and you'll marvel at more than eighty whimsical living sculptures—giraffes, elephants, bears, even a unicorn—each meticulously cared for just as they have been for more than a century.

Green Animals Topiary Garden
380 Cory's Ln., Portsmouth, RI 02871
(401) 847-1000
newportmansions.org/explore/green-animals-topiary-garden

TIP
The second floor of the Brayton estate home houses a collection of antique toys, if you're looking for even more childlike wonder.

WAVE THE FLAG
AT BRISTOL'S FOURTH OF JULY PARADE

The annual Fourth of July Parade in Bristol is the oldest in America, and quite the grand old procession it is. First observed in 1785, the parade runs for two miles through downtown Bristol, attracting fifty thousand-plus spectators, including residents who throw big house parties along the parade route for friends and family. Officially the "Military, Civic and Fireman's Parade," the Fourth of July Parade features uniformed first responders from all across the state as well as members of the armed forces, musket-firing militia groups, marching bands, fire trucks, military vehicles, floats, bagpipers, and marchers dressed in every red, white, and blue ensemble imaginable. Arrive early if you want to set up a chair to enjoy the show: from Bristol's small-town charm to the heartfelt expressions of patriotism, this is the best place to celebrate Independence Day in Rhode Island.

fourthofjulybristolri.com

TIP
Avoid the traffic into Bristol by parking out of town and use pedal power to get into town with a ride along the East Bay Bike Path.

FIND YOUR
COUNTRY SOUL
AT THE WASHINGTON COUNTY FAIR

Here's a little secret about Rhode Island: while the cities like Newport and Providence get a lot of attention, most of the state is rural, not urban. And while it will never be mistaken for Iowa or Kansas, Rhode Island has more than 1,200 working farms and an agricultural heritage dating back to the seventeenth century (the state's official name, for example, is the State of Rhode Island and Providence Plantations). That's a long way of explaining why the Washington County Fair is a legit agricultural fair, not some cow and pony show put on for tourists. For more than fifty years the fair, held in Richmond, has awarded ribbons for animal husbandry and horticulture, hosted a carnival midway and live country music acts, run tractor pulls and cow pie-tossing contests, and offered a rich variety of food from concession stands run by local civic groups.

Washington County Fair
78 Richmond Townhouse Rd. (Rte. 112), Richmond, RI 02812
washingtoncountyfair-ri.com

TIP
Bring some folding chairs so you'll have a place
to set a spell when the bands take the stage.

GRAB THE BRASS RING
AT THE CRESCENT PARK CAROUSEL

"Grabbing the brass ring" isn't just an idiom at this classic merry-go-round located on the former grounds of Riverside's Crescent Park amusement park. The roller coaster, sky ride, and shore dining hall have all vanished, but the park's Charles I. D. Looff-designed carousel spins on. Built in 1895 and featuring sixty-one hand-carved animals and four chariots, the carousel retains its original German band organ, and riders can still reach out to grasp a brass ring as they spin around (a free ride is the reward). Kids and adults alike are welcome to climb onto the back of their favorite steed (or the one camel) for just two dollars. The onion-domed hippodrome building housing the carousel is also original to Crescent Park, making this experience a true step back into time.

700 Bullocks Point Ave., Riverside, RI 02915
(401) 435-7518
crescentparkcarousel.org

TIP
Visit the carousel on Friday nights during the summer and stay for free Movies in the Park, featuring classic Disney and children's films.

PARK YOURSELF IN WESTERLY
FOR LIVE SHAKESPEARE

"Over park, over pale, / Thorough flood, thorough fire, / I do wander everywhere." Thus wrote William Shakespeare in *A Midsummer Night's Dream*, and while he wasn't actually encouraging readers to come see his best works at Westerly's Wilcox Park, it's definitely something you need to wander down to on at least one midsummer night. Presented annually by the Colonial Theatre, Shakespeare in the Park features one of the Bard's plays each season, staged Tuesday through Sunday nights at 8 p.m. in late July and early August. Free to attend, the production attracts thousands of theater-lovers to beautiful Wilcox Park, formally designed by Warren H. Manning, an associate of landscaping legend Frederick Law Olmstead, and located in the heart of beautiful downtown Westerly.

Shakespeare in the Park
Wilcox Park, 44 Broad St., Westerly, RI 02891
colonialtheatreri.org

TIP
Bring a blanket, some snacks, and perhaps some "invisible spirit" (as Shakespeare might say) to make an evening at the theater even merrier.

EXPLORE THE RUINS
AT FORT WETHERILL

From Colonial times through World War II, forts have stood on the one-hundred-foot cliffs at the east end of Conanicut (Jamestown) Island to protect Narragansett Bay from invading warships and, later, submarines. Fort Wetherill was the last of these, a massive concrete bunker bristling with coastal defense weapons, including twelve-inch artillery pieces mounted on disappearing tracks for defensive purposes. The military abandoned the fort in 1946 and the big guns are long gone, but it's been a rite of passage for generations of Rhode Island kids to explore the crumbling and graffiti-covered ruins of the fort. The old gun emplacements remain visible, and the views of the bay from the top of the fortress remain impressive; bold visitors may also venture into the dark, damp rooms below, where tracks once used to bring heavy shells to the guns still hang from the ceilings.

Fort Wetherill
Fort Wetherill Rd., Jamestown, RI 02835
riparks.com/locations/locationfortwetherill.html

TIP

Fort Getty, a sister gun emplacement in Jamestown, has a campground where you can pitch a tent steps from the shore of Narragansett Bay for just thirty dollars a night.

SEE THE TORAH
AT TOURO SYNAGOGUE

Newport's historic district is home to the oldest Jewish house of worship in the United States. Touro Synagogue on Spring Street was built in 1763, more than a century after the first Jews arrived in the city from Barbados. In perhaps his most definitive statement on religious liberty, President George Washington wrote to the Touro congregants in 1790 to assure them that the newborn United States "gives to bigotry no sanction, to persecution no assistance, requires only that they who live under its protection should demean themselves as good citizens, in giving it on all occasions their effectual support." Visitors can tour the sanctuary and see the ark and the synagogue's Torah scrolls; a historic Jewish cemetery and a visitor's center are nearby.

Touro Synagogue
85 Touro St., Newport, RI 02840
tourosynagogue.org

TIP
Each August the congregation holds a ceremonial reading of Washington's letter to honor its message of freedom and inclusion; past guest speakers have included Supreme Court Justices Ruth Bader Ginsberg and Elena Kagan.

ENJOY TOURS AND TUNES
AT FORT ADAMS

Despite never having delivered or received a shot fired in anger, Newport's Fort Adams is an impressive place. Built beginning in 1824, the thick-walled fortification guarded Narragansett Bay from the threat of southern raiders during the U.S. Civil War and temporarily housed the U.S. Naval Academy. It remained an active part of New England's coastal defenses until World War II. The fort is now the centerpiece of Fort Adams State Park, most famously the site of the annual Newport Folk Festival and the Newport Jazz Festival, and the Fort Adams Trust runs tours of the battlements, tunnels, and officers' quarters. The trust also leads golf cart tours of the grounds outside the fort, including a stop at the former "Summer White House" of President Dwight D. Eisenhower.

Fort Adams
90 Fort Adams Dr., Fort Adams State Park, Newport, RI 02840
(401) 841-0707
fortadams.org

TIP
Try to visit around Halloween, when a haunted house called the Fortress of Nightmares is staged within the tunnels of the old fort.

FALL IN LOVECRAFT
WITH PROVIDENCE'S MASTER OF LITERARY HORROR

Horror writer H. P. Lovecraft was born and died in Providence and wrote his most famous works in the city. Visitors to Providence can connect with the creator of the monstrous Cthulhu and the magical textbook *The Necronomicon* by visiting his former home at 10 Barnes Street and his gravesite in historic Swan Point Cemetery ("I Am Providence," a memorial marker proclaims) or dropping in at the Lovecraft Arts & Sciences Council bookstore in the historic Arcade building downtown, which sponsors readings and book signings by authors of "weird fiction." The Council also produces NecronomiCon, a biennial conference that includes expert discussions, gaming, films, and other activities inspired by Lovecraft's haunting works—appropriately, NecronomiCon is held during odd-numbered years.

Lovecraft Arts & Sciences Council
65 Weybosset St., Providence, RI 02903
(401) 454-4568
weirdprovidence.org
necronomicon-providence.com
arcadeprovidence.com

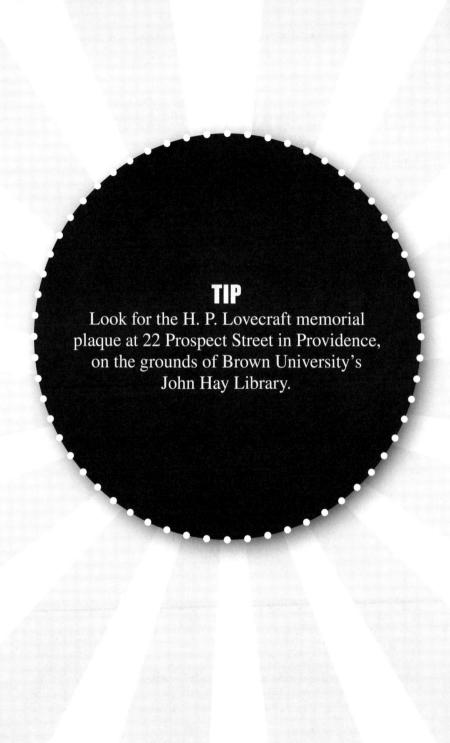

TIP
Look for the H. P. Lovecraft memorial
plaque at 22 Prospect Street in Providence,
on the grounds of Brown University's
John Hay Library.

STROLL (OR JOG)
THROUGH THE SWAN POINT CEMETERY

Cemeteries can be strangely beautiful places, and that description certainly fits Providence's Swan Point Cemetery. Established in 1846 on the banks of the Seekonk River, the sixty-acre cemetery is the final resting place for macabre author H. P. Lovecraft, Civil War General Ambrose Burnside, Sullivan Ballou (who penned a memorable love letter to his wife shortly before being killed at the Battle of Bull Run), and a virtual who's-who of prominent Rhode Islanders. Listed on the National Register of Historic Places, the two-hundred-acre cemetery is known for its elaborately carved nineteenth-century memorials. Visitors are welcome to walk (or take an early morning jog) along the cemetery's network of footpaths—just be quiet and respectful, since this is still a working cemetery and a place of mourning and solemn reflection.

Swan Point Cemetery
585 Blackstone Blvd., Providence, RI 02906
(401) 272-1314
swanpointcemetery.com

TIP
Weary walkers can take a seat in the riverside gazebo called Stranger's Rest, originally built in 1887 by Sarah Anthony in memory of her husband, Benjamin.

CELEBRATE CHRISTMAS
AT THE MANSIONS

Newport's famous Bellevue Avenue mansions were built (apparently without irony) as seaside "summer cottages" by some of the wealthiest families in nineteenth-century America. Marble House, Breakers, The Elms, and seven other remarkable homes are maintained by the Preservation Society of Newport County, which runs tours covering everything from the life of the servants who worked in the mansions to the hidden technology that helped keep the houses running. Tours are offered year-round, but the mansions shine brightest during the holiday season when they are decorated with Christmas trees, wreaths, lights, and vintage toys. Kids can visit with Santa Claus, while some mansions have special evening openings with live holiday music and holiday treats like eggnog, cider, and cookies.

newportmansions.org

TIP

The Island Moving Company traditionally presents *The Newport Nutcracker at Rosecliff* in the Rosecliff mansion, with the home's ballroom, salons, and grand staircase setting the stage for a merry night of ballet.

EXPERIENCE GEMÜTLICHKEIT
AT THE GERMAN AMERICAN CULTURAL SOCIETY

Rhode Island's diverse ethnicity has blessed the state with an abundance of social clubs and civic groups—the Polish, Portuguese, Italians, and Greeks all have gathering places of their own, just to name a few. One of the coolest, though, is Pawtucket's German American Cultural Society of Rhode Island, which, in addition to offering German language lessons and sponsoring traditional dance groups, operates a genuine Bavarian beer hall and Rathskeller. The latter is open every Friday night (you don't have to be German or a society member to visit) and serves German food—five varieties of wurst plus sauerkraut, potato salad, and pretzels, as well as occasional special dishes—and beer on tap from breweries like Weihenstephan, Warsteiner, Franziskaner, and Radeberger. You'll get extra "respekt" if you arrive wearing lederhosen or a dirndl.

German American Cultural Society
78 Carter Ave., Pawtucket, RI 02861
(401) 726-9873
gacsri.org

TIP

The society's Oktoberfest celebration features an outdoor beer garden and polka oompah bands playing on the beer hall stage.

CATCH A FLICK
AT THE AVON CINEMA

The Avon Cinema's Art Deco marquee reveals the movie theater's roots—this single-screener has been a fixture on Thayer Street in Providence since 1938. The longevity is remarkable on an avenue where businesses come and go seemingly in response to the whim of every passing class of Brown University students, but the appeal of the Avon—which shows "first run foreign and domestic films of distinction"—endures. Maybe it's the old-school jingles enticing moviegoers to the snack bar, the real butter on the popcorn, or the personal greeting you get at the door that doesn't happen in the multiplex down the road. Or perhaps it's just the joy of sharing a dark space for a couple of hours with other people for whom going to the movies is a passion, not a diversion. Whatever way the magic happens, seeing a movie at the Avon is a throwback experience to cherish.

Avon Cinema
260 Thayer St., Providence, RI 02906
(401) 421-0020
avoncinema.com

TIP
With the sad demise of Providence's Cable Car Cinema, the Avon has picked up the torch of showing the Academy Award-winning animated and short subject films each Oscar season.

SPRING INTO
THE ST. PATRICK'S DAY PARADE IN NEWPORT

Newport is known to tourists primarily as a summer town, but the locals know that the real time to emerge from hibernation is in mid-March for the city's annual St. Patrick's Day Parade. Rain, shine, or snow, thousands line the sidewalks of Thames Street (and even more crowd the city's bars and restaurants) beginning at 9 a.m., usually with a wee dram of Irish whiskey or Guinness to ward off the spring morning chill. A Newport tradition for more than sixty years, the parade moves in a swirl of green and the sound of bagpipes and includes participation from local politicians, civic groups, mini Shriner cars, clowns, jugglers, and unicyclists. It's as much a party as a parade, and one that continues long after the last marchers leave the street.

newportirish.com

TIP
The parade is always held on the Saturday prior to St. Patrick's Day (March 17). Also, public drinking is technically illegal in Newport, making pretty much every adult at the parade a lawbreaker of some sort.

LEARN ABOUT THE INDUSTRIAL REVOLUTION
AT SLATER MILL

Samuel Slater was a typical denizen of a state that's long been semi-affectionately dubbed "Rogue's Island": when he wanted to kickstart his business, he essentially swiped the technology for his mill from his native England and set up shop in Pawtucket. The big gamble paid off—Slater is now known as the father of the American Industrial Revolution, and his 1793 textile mill still stands on the banks of the Blackstone River, which once provided the water power needed to run its looms. The mill, along with the nearby Wilkinson Mill and the period Sylvanus Brown House, is now a National Historic Landmark and is open for tours; you can walk the floor of the stone mill to see the revolutionary carding system invented by Slater, learn from guides about the lives of the people (including children) who worked the looms, and see the waters of the Blackstone roaring over the Slater Mill Dam.

Slater Mill
67 Roosevelt Ave., Pawtucket, RI 02860
nps.gov/blac/index.htm

TIP

Make a stop at Slater Mill as part of a tour of the Blackstone River Valley National Heritage Corridor, which includes the Museum of Work and Culture in Woonsocket.

HONOR NATIVE CULTURE
AT THE CHARLESTOWN POWWOW

The oldest recorded Native American powwow isn't held out west somewhere, but right here in Rhode Island. For more than 340 years, the Narragansett tribe has been gathering on their ancestral lands in Charlestown to celebrate their culture, and a tribe that famously welcomed state founder Roger Williams with open arms still invites visitors to attend. Traditional dancing by tribal members is always a highlight of the August powwow, which also features Native American food, crafts, and music and opens with a Grand Entry procession led by the Chief Sachem of the Narragansetts. Members of other local tribes like the Wampanoags also take part in the gathering on the ground of the historic Narragansett Indian Church, which dates to 1859.

Narragansett Indian Tribe Powwow
Indian Church Rd., Charlestown, RI 02813
(401) 364-1105
narragansett-tribe.org

TIP
Learn more about Narragansett tribal history at the Tomaquag Museum in Exeter.

GET THE FIRST GIFT OF CHRISTMAS
ON THE POLAR EXPRESS

The Providence and Worcester Railroad spends most of the year delivering freight, but every holiday season it opens up its tracks to a magical train ride that recreates the classic Christmas story *The Polar Express*, written by Rhode Island native Chris Van Allsburg. If you've read the book or seen the Tom Hanks movie, you know that the story revolves around a young boy who jumps aboard a steam train on Christmas Eve for an enchanted journey to meet Santa at the North Pole. Passengers holding a golden ticket on the Blackstone Valley Polar Express train take a similar one-and-a-half-hour trip that includes a reading of the story, cookies and hot chocolate, holiday songs, and of course meeting Santa, who gives each child the first gift of Christmas, just like in the book.

Blackstone Valley Polar Express
blackstonevalleypolarexpress.com

TIP
Polar Express passengers are encouraged to wear their pajamas on the train.

Savoy Bookshop and Café (Photo credit: Katherine Gendreau)

SHOPPING AND FASHION

CURL UP WITH A GOOD BOOK
AT THE SAVOY

C. S. Lewis famously said, "You can never get a cup of tea large enough or a book long enough to suit me." At Westerly's elegant bookstore Savoy, you can get both the book and the brew (coffee, too). In an era when it seemed like Amazon and big-box booksellers were going to kill off local bookstores for good, along came this audacious literary shrine in 2016—two endlessly delightful floors of a former hotel filled with books and nooks to read them in. The Savoy Café will provide the caffeine you need to get through that one more chapter, and there's always an event going on when you need to give your eyes a rest—author luncheons and book signings, book club meetings, poetry readings, and story hour for kids, to name a few. Mostly the Savoy just exudes warmth and a welcome to those who understand that a book really is "a dream you hold in your hands."

Savoy Bookshop and Café
10 Canal St., Westerly, RI 02891
(401) 213-3901
banksquarebooks.com/westerly-store

TIP
Support local and self-published authors
by browsing the titles in the Savoy's
consignment section.

PICK APPLES
AT JASWELL'S FARM

Rhode Island has about a dozen orchards where you can pick apples in season, but the annual fall tradition is embraced most firmly at Jaswell's Farm in Smithfield, the heart of Rhode Island's apple country. You can pick your own apples here in September and October, and the farm also produces its own fresh apple cider, gourmet and candy apples, apple pies, and fresh cider doughnuts (doughboys and french fries are also on the menu to fuel your apple-picking adventure). The family farm, founded in 1899, cultivates a wide variety of apples over the course of the season, including Honeycrisp, McIntosh, Cortland, Gala, Golden Delicious, Empire, Macoun, Mutsu, and Pink Lady.

Jaswell's Farm
50 Swan Rd., Smithfield, RI 02917
(401) 231-9043
jaswellsfarm.com

TIP

Apple-picking season overlaps with pumpkin season, so you can get ready for Halloween decorating while priming your sweet tooth with cider doughnuts.

COMMUNE WITH ARTISTS
AT THE FANTASTIC UMBRELLA FACTORY

Walking onto the grounds of this rustic complex of shops and galleries feels like stepping back in time—specifically, to a hippie colony in the sixties. In fact, the Fantastic Umbrella Factory was founded in 1968 as an emporium selling penny candy and unique goods. While the original store is no longer in business, visitors can still walk through the lush gardens, visit the resident goats and emus, and browse through about a half-dozen shops and an artist loft. The new General Store sells some of the same toys and treats as the old emporium, while Small Axe Productions, Frills, and Axiom are imbued with a counterculture groove as well. As it was intended from the beginning, Charlestown's Fantastic Umbrella Factory is an oasis of timeless serenity.

Fantastic Umbrella Factory
4820 Old Post Rd., Charlestown, RI 02813
(401) 364-1060
fantasticumbrellafactory.com

TIP

The Small Axe Cafe serves lunch using only locally sourced organic goods, and you can bring your own wine to sip in the dining room or garden while you nosh.

SAY HOW NOW, COW
AT WRIGHT'S DAIRY FARM & BAKERY

Most Americans have little conception of where their food comes from or how it's produced, and that's true of milk, too. At Wright's Dairy Farm & Bakery, not only can you buy milk fresh from the cow and delicious ice cream, but you also can watch the cows being milked and take a tour to learn about the farm's production process, which includes pasteurizing and bottling the milk. Visitors can also see baby cows and shop at the bakery and cake shop, where the cannoli and cream puffs are made using the farm's own milk and cream. Like any good Rhode Island bakery, Wright's also sells pizza strips—cheese and no-cheese varieties—but is probably most famous for its Hermits—an old-fashioned style of cookie made with molasses, spices, and raisins.

Wright's Dairy Farm & Bakery
200 Woonsocket Hill Rd., North Smithfield, RI 02896
(401) 767-3014
wrightsdairyfarm.com

TIP
If you want to see the cows get milked, visit any day between 3 p.m. and 4:30 p.m.

PICK UP SOME TREASURES
AT THE WICKFORD ART FESTIVAL

The sleepy coastal village of Wickford rouses itself modestly when summer visitors come to town, but it really comes most to life in mid-July, when it plays host to the Wickford Art Festival. Artists set up tents and exhibit their paintings, sculptures, and other works up and down the streets of this pint-sized town. It's a pretty egalitarian event—you can spend five dollars on a work of art or $5,000, depending on your taste and budget. The festival, sponsored by the Wickford Art Association, has been held for more than half a century and draws two hundred-plus regional, national, and international artists. Local student artists also have an opportunity to exhibit their works, and the food concession run by the First Baptist Church helps the event retain its small-town character.

Wickford Art Festival
wickfordart.org

EXPERIENCE SENSORY OVERLOAD
IN WARREN'S IMAGINE GIFT STORE

The building housing the Imagine Gift Store in Warren was once the Lyric Theatre, but it's unlikely that the old movie house ever staged anything quite as dazzling as the gift shop that now occupies its former auditorium, mezzanine, and balcony. The explosion of pastel color on the outside of the building is nearly matched by the kaladescope of merchandise sold within, including food produced at local culinary collaborative Hope & Main, nautical jewelry, toys and games, "Life is Good" and Rhode Island branded clothing, and souvenirs that include coffee syrup and Del's Lemonade mix. You can also satisfy your sweet tooth with forty flavors of saltwater taffy, rock candy, and other sweet treats in the Candy Shoppe as well as a variety of hard ice cream flavors served in waffle cones in the Ice Cream Shop.

Imagine Gift Store
5 Miller St., Warren, RI 02885
(401) 245-4200
giftimagine.com

TIP

Stop for a selfie with one of the four full-sized cow statues at the store, created by artists as entries in international Cow Parade charitable events.

Beavertail light (Photo credit: Paul Kandarian)

SUGGESTED
ITINERARIES

DATE NIGHT

Light Up the Night at *WaterFire*, 124

Get Into a Grilled Pizza at Al Forno, 28

Catch a Flick at the Avon Cinema, 150

Make a Comedy Connection in East Providence, 43

Stock Up on Musicals at Theatre By The Sea, 122

Drink In Summer on the Castle Hill Inn's Lawn, 27

Invade the Hotel Viking Rooftop for Drinks and Dining, 18

Tune In to Live Music at the Greenwich Odeum, 50

PUB CRAWL

Sea a Band Play at the Ocean Mist, 40

Hit the Block for Summer Concerts at Ballard's, 47

Experience Gemütlichkeit at the German American Cultural Society, 148

Get Spirited at Sons of Liberty, 12

Enjoy Burgers, Bands, and Bocce at the Rathskeller, 32

Toast the Sunset on the Coast Guard House Deck, 26

Punch Your Passport on the Rhode Island Brewery Trail, 14

FOR THE KIDS

AUTHENTICALLY RHODE ISLAND

BY THE SEA

Sail a 12 Metre Yacht in Newport Harbor, 118

Camp on the Sand at East Beach, 114

Join a Summer Float Party on Narragansett Bay, 108

Spot a Snowy Owl at Sachuest Point, 55

GET ACTIVE

Get Rugged on the Newport Cliff Walk, 72

Tour the East Bay by Pedal Power, 60

Stroll (or Jog) through the Swan Point Cemetery, 146

Gallop in the Surf on Block Island, 59

Climb Neutaconkanut Hill, 107

Go Karting in Lincoln, 66

Kayak the Narrow River, 100

Prepare for Awe on the Trestle Trail, 73

Bike the Block, 62

ACTIVITIES
BY SEASON

WINTER

Celebrate Christmas at the Mansions, 147

Take a Snowy Slide at Yawgoo Valley Ski Area, 82

Get Scrooged at Trinity Rep's *A Christmas Carol*, 130

Roar with the Crowd at a Providence Bruins Game, 80

Get the First Gift of Christmas on the Polar Express, 155

Skate in Kennedy Plaza, 102

SPRING

Step Out to Rhode Island's Best Waterfall, 103

Tap into Your Sweet Side at the Spring Hill Sugar House, 9

Spring into the St. Patrick's Day Parade in Newport, 151

Attend a May Breakfast, 4

Fish for Stripers on Narragansett Bay, 104

SUMMER

Saddle Up for Newport Polo, 54

Get Wild at Paddy's in Westerly, 20

Wave the Flag at Bristol's Fourth of July Parade, 135

Catch a Game at Cardines Field, 56

Beach It at the Mohegan Bluffs, 74

Attend the Newport Folk and Jazz Festivals, 42

FALL

INDEX